In My Fashion is 'an evocative and enjoyable account of a bygone era. It's neither nostalgic nor whimsical but affectionately remembers the past as it was. There's a great deal of humour and a rich array of characters.'

Jenny Stephens, BBC Radio Drama Producer

Generations of women toiled in Leicester's hosiery factories. This is the story of one of them, a school leaver who started work cutting cotton vests for the Cherub factory in 1949, then went on to work in a dress factory and progressed to the design office.

Highlights in her life at this time included Saturday nights at the Palais wearing Max Factor makeup, weekends hiking to youth hostels, and listening to talk about sex. They are all described with matter of fact humour and innocence.

But this story is not just about one person's factory life – it's about everyone who gets a job, grows up and tries to figure everything out.

Mary Essinger's previous publications:

Wounded Bird of Paradise   a novel

Only When I Laugh   comedy scripts

IN MY FASHION

Starting work in the heyday of
Leicester's knitwear factories

Mary Essinger

*With best wishes
from
Mary E*

Heart of Albion

IN MY FASHION:

Starting work in the heyday of Leicester's knitwear factories

Mary Essinger

Some names have been changed.

ISBN 1 872883 79 6

© Copyright Mary Essinger 2005

Published by

Heart of Albion Press
2 Cross Hill Close, Wymeswold
Loughborough, LE12 6UJ

albion@indigogroup.co.uk

Visit our Web site: www.hoap.co.uk

Printed in England by Booksprint

For Christen

Contents

Acknowledgements

Terri Bradshaw and Ann Thornton for illustrations

David Foister

Thelma Davis (née Claffey)

Pat Ractliffe (née Tempest)

Mike Harper

Jenny Stephens

Record Office for Leicester, Leicestershire and Rutland

members of Leicester Writers' Club members for their enthusiastic support

THE UNDERWEAR FACTORY

My first job was at an underwear factory. After climbing the stone stairs there was a huge clock face with about two hundred numbers round its rim. After selecting my card from the rack on the wall I had to turn the arm of the clock till it reached my number and then punch in the time of arrival. Clocking in for somebody else meant getting the sack on the spot.

We all had to get clocked on by 8 am. Right on the dot of eight o'clock the doors were locked and not opened again till quarter-past. Anyone who arrived later than quarter-past had to go in, shame-faced, by the front door, at half-past.

This lockout system was to make workers prompt, which it probably did, but meant lost wages and a fifteen-minute wait in the cold if the tram happened to be late. I could never see the point of a lockout system – if workers were needed why keep them outside?

At that time, in 1948, jobs were advertised in the *Mercury* in two or three long columns under 'Hosiery Operatives' and sub-headed 'Cutters', 'Menders', 'Overlockers' and other operations. Some said 'School Leavers Welcome'.

'School leavers' then meant fourteen-year olds and that 's how old I was when I first encountered the factory of Arthur Foister's Cherub works on Charles Street on a sunny September morning wearing a new dirndl skirt and carrying a school report. I walked in through the front entrance, the only time I would ever see it except when I was late. Standing in the oak panelled vestibule I pressed a bell that said, 'Please ring for attention'. A hatch opened like a speakeasy and a girl not much older than me said in a superior way, "Wait here for the forelady."

The Cherub factory in Charles Street. Coronation Year, 1953.

The forelady wore a white overall and I followed her to a small room and stood while she sat making notes at a desk. She took down my age, name and address and asked questions.

Forelady	"Have you ever used a sewing machine?"
Me	"Yes, I make my own clothes."
Forelady	"Did you make that skirt?"
Me	"No, I bought it specially… "
Forelady	"Well, specially for what?"
Me	"For this interview."
Forelady	"When you make your own clothes do you cut them out yourself?"
Me	"Yes."
Forelady	"Start on Monday, back entrance. The normal time is eight o'clock but, on your first day only, you start at nine. Ask for Mrs Wells in the cutting room on the top floor. The rate is twenty-five shillings weekly and you will be paid a week in hand."

She didn't ask to see my school report but I was glad to get out into the street because my new skirt was too loose and needed hitching up.

* * *

Me	"What does a week in hand mean?"
Mother	"It means there's no pay the first week. You will be paid at the end of the second week for the work you did on the first."
Me	"But when do I get the second week's money?"
Mother	"Not till you leave."

It was all very hard to understand.

* * *

All I could see was a huge room with long wooden tables sectioned off into individual benches about five yards long. The people in the room, at first glance, all looked the same. About fifty women and girls were facing each other as they walked up and down the benches cutting white cloth.

I stood in the doorway wearing a raincoat over a summer dress. I stood a long time. Nearby a woman was stretching so far over her counter that her feet were nearly off the ground. Se saw me watching and, breathless, said, "Are you waiting for Mrs Wells?"

I nodded.

"Nellie," she shouted down the room, "you're wanted."

From far away I heard another voice shouting, "Nellie, you're wanted." After this came yet another shout, "Tell her she's too early."

The first woman relayed the answer to me, "Nellie says you're too early. Wait a bit."

When she appeared, Mrs Wells, an old woman of about forty-five in a pink overall, showed me the cloakroom.

Mrs Wells   "Leave your coat here every day, outdoor clothes are not to be worn in the workroom. You can't smoke in here. There's the toilets and you can't smoke in there either."

From fabric knitted on circular machines on the ground floor, the factory produced white cotton vests and pants for men and boys but first I had to learn how to use shears. Mrs Wells took me to side table where there were some lengths of cloth. After laying one layer on top of another she took a six-inch metal square and drew round it four times with blue chalk.

Mrs Wells   "Watch how I cut them out, keep the shears flat, see, and keep the lines straight. Carry on cutting squares and I'll be back after break."

I pulled up a stool.

Mrs Wells   "What are you doing? You don't sit down to cut, you stand."

I couldn't keep the fabric layers together at first and the shears were hurting my thumb. Then I spotted Thelma, who used to be at my school and she waved. It was wonderful to see somebody I knew. She came across.

Thelma   "Why are you cutting already?"

Me   "That's where they sent me."

Thelma   "Aren't you going to be a runabout then?"

Me   "What's a runabout?"

Thelma   "All new ones start as runabouts fetching and carrying from one floor to another."

Me   "What's the point of that?"

Thelma   "They get to know the factory, they find out what they want to do. I've got to get back to my bench, see you at break."

Me   "What's the break?"

Thelma   "You'll hear the trolley, we all queue up. You get a cup of tea and a sit down."

After break Mrs Wells inspected my work, sniffing with disapproval at the crooked lines.

Mrs Wells   "This looks as if it's been cut with a knife and fork. One cut with your shear, not three and don't make so much waste between the squares. Watch me carefully."

Like lightning she marked up more squares slicing through the fabric so fast I could hardly see how she did it.

By the end of the week I was cutting circles and laying up five layers. Thelma showed me how to make myself a half-moon shaped leather apron to tie round my waist so I didn't wear my dress out when it rubbed on the bench.

Finally Mrs Wells began to show me how to cut vests and pants like a proper cutter. First I had to pull fabric from a roll and billow it in the air like waves before laying it along the bench loosely to relax the fabric while I examined it for flaws.

Mrs Wells   "Everything you cut must be perfect, bad machining can be put right but if anything is cut wrong it's ruined, so cutting is very important."

The cloth smelt oily and sometimes a seed of cotton was caught in the fibre making an uneven bump. I had to mark these faults.

After examining the fabric I pushed it back to one side ready to lay the first layer along the bench. Three or four more layers were spread over it with all edges precisely level and all the time keeping note of the position of flaws.

Then I laid the metal pattern on with its cut out shape of necklines and armholes and drew round it with a triangle of chalk; I'd seen the girls sharpening chalk with the edge of their shears. I had to cut by pressing on the top of the shears as they scrunched through the layers. It was hard at first but Mrs Wells showed me how to wrap strips of cloth round the handles for comfort. Then the work was tied up in bundles of one dozen and I had to sign the ticket where it said 'Cutter'.

Eventually, when I was fast enough, I went on piecework and was paid, not by the week, but by the number of garments produced. Although office work was considered ladylike and superior, factory pay was much better, and piecework was best of all.

Older worker   "The women here don't dress up. They don't put money on their backs but they've all got lovely homes."

Some work paid better than others, little vests, for example, paid the same as big ones but little vests were quicker to cut. Even in shops today men's large vests cost the same as small ones but use twice as much fabric.

If the fabric had too many faults the foreman was called over and he sometimes allowed extra time for that batch.

Cutting was always done standing up. Nobody can stand still all day but walking along the bench was not tiring

Every Friday I took my shears home for extra sharpening. These shears, strictly for cutting cloth, and never paper, were guarded carefully, and no worker ever used anyone else's shears.

Friend   "Why is your finger hard down one side?"

Me   "That's where the shears rub against the skin."

Friend   "I wouldn't ever do any job that spoiled my fingers."

At twelve o'clock it was home to dinner, on bikes, on foot or by bus. Dinner was a cooked meal, with my three brothers and Mum and Dad. One brother was still at school and the other two were serving apprenticeships in printing; apprenticeships for boys, factories for girls. We listened to 'Workers' Playtime' on the Light Programme. These were live outside broadcasts from various factories and featured music, a comedian and a soprano usually singing 'One Fine Day' from *Madame Butterfly*. The broadcasts ended with community singing, and I returned to work at 1 p.m..

It was always called 'dinner,' lunch was something in a paper bag in your pocket for tea break.

A girl named Betty lived far away in the country at Markfield on a duck farm and I asked how she got home every day.

Betty   "I don't go home. I have my dinner at Sylvia's house. She lives on
            Uppingham Road so it's near."

Me   "What's it like there?"

Betty   "Very posh. They have side plates and as soon as we get in we
            have a cup of tea. I pay of course, I pay once a week."

Back at work after dinner girls would call to each other:

"What did you have today?"

"Liver and onions, how about you?"

"Toad in the hole and rhubarb roly-poly."

"I love jam roly-poly, raspberry jam's my favourite."

I thought it strange to talk about food in this way, in our house it was
considered gluttonous to talk about food. It was easy to chat to each other as
we worked because, apart from the scrunch of shears, the cutting area was
quiet. Girls who had been to the pictures the previous night would relate, at
length, the whole plot as they worked and it was impossible to keep track of
the story:

"Then he said to her, then she said to the other man, then they
went back to the forest and that first man was waiting with a gun
and before that…"

Bosses were shadowy figures who appeared in the workroom when there
were problems. The two sons were called Mr David and Mr Roger and their
father was Arthur Foister. These bosses were the only people in the factory
who wore suits, usually navy and pin-striped. Clothes worn in the factory were
markers of status. Workers wore old clothes and office staff dressed nicely. If
a girl appeared looking smart under her overall she was bombarded with
comments.

"Going out straight from work?"

"Who is he then?"

"I bet you think you look nice in that."

Wearing hair curlers all day under a scarf was another sign you were 'going out straight from work.'

Each afternoon at around 3 o'clock, everybody started singing. I never knew how it began, it just seemed to happen, and every day the songs were the same. Not pop songs, not pub songs but old ballads of the kind found in a poetry anthology under the heading 'Traditional Anonymous.' This piece began the singing:

> 'Where have you been all day Henry my son,
> Where have you been all day my beloved one?
> In the meadow, in the meadow.'
> Make my bed there's a pain in my head
> And I want to lie down and die.
> What will you leave your mother Henry my son
> What will you leave your mother my beloved one?
> Silks and satins, silks and satins.
> Make my bed there's a pain in my head
> And I want to lie down and die.
> What will you leave your father Henry my son,
> What will you leave your father my beloved one?
> A rope to hang him, a rope to hang him.
> Make my bed there's a pain in my head
> And I want to lie down and die."

There are others verses now forgotten and it occurs to me that this song may have been part of a tradition of women singing at work and could have been passed down through the generations. It may also, like many ballads, have chronicled an actual event.

Everybody sang except for one, a girl named Linda, a girl who considered herself above us. Nellie, as I now called Mrs Wells, told us Linda took private singing lessons.

1940s birthday card.

Me	"Linda never joins in the singing."
Mother	"Why not?"
Me	"It will spoil her voice because she's a colly tora soprano."
Mother	"Gracie Fields was a coloratura, she used to sing in the factory, so why can't Linda?"

On your birthday you were supposed to provide iced buns for everybody, passing them round in a lid from a big cardboard box. For my birthday I took petite fours instead, reduced price, from a posh bakers; they were not pleased about that ("You're supposed to bring buns with lemon icing on them"). I thought the petite fours were much prettier than buns.

Friday was pay day and late in the afternoon we gathered at the top of the room to wait for Mrs Jackson in her white overall.

Mike Harper's first wage slip from 2nd January 1953.

Tax Week No............ending.................................19......

Name .... *Mr Harper.*

Salary ...   . £ *2 : 5 : 0*

<u>Deductions</u>

Income Tax   £   :   :

Insurance   : *3 : 5*

Pension Sch,   :   : £ *. : 3 : 5*

Nett £ *2 : 1 : 4*

She stood with a tray of small brown packets and when she called our name we stepped forward to collect our wages.

The Friday before the annual holiday we collected two week's wages. Whatever we earned the week before, up to Wednesday, was doubled by Foisters for holiday pay. All week we'd worked non-stop, with hardly a break, in order to boost our output and earn extra. The name for this was 'scratting.' Scratting was frowned on normally because it could undermine the rate for a job but everybody scratted at holiday time.

This wage packet with holiday pay gave me a tremendous feeling of excitement. This was the biggest amount of money I had ever held in my hand and all the things I wanted were suddenly in my grasp. It was a sense of power and freedom, of having money to splash out on anything. No windfall since, no legacy, no prize money, has ever made me feel as wealthy as the thrill of that bulging wage packet.

BEFORE SEX WAS INVENTED

At home, while my brother giggled over Goya nudes on the Spanish stamps in his collection, I read the *News of the World*, a newspaper devoured in our house every Sunday. This was real life. Especially instructive were breach of promise cases where a woman, under promise of marriage 'anticipated the wedding night,' and the man was in court for failing to keep his promise to marry her. The judge usually awarded money to the woman, especially, but not necessarily, if there was a baby involved. This breach of promise law, which was repealed soon afterwards, was puzzling. What would have happened if the man in court had said to the judge, "All right, I don't want to, but I'll marry her?"

The talk of the cutting room was a girl named Julie who was engaged to be married.

Me	"Julie Watson's brought her wedding forward to July instead of October."
Mother	"Oh yes… "
Me	"And it's going to be in the registry office."
Mother	"She's having a baby."
Me	"Oh no. The church was fully booked."
Mother	"She's having baby you'll see. And when it's born she'll say it's premature. When you get married it'll be in a church and I want you to wear a white dress. You know what I mean."

The talk of the whole factory was a new worker named Mandy in the mending section. Word went round that she told everybody she'd been to bed with her boyfriend. Going to bed with a boyfriend was shameful enough but talking about it openly was unheard of. One by one we left our benches and wandered into the mending section on pretend business to look at her.

Me   "She looks quite normal."

Jean   "Common. Too much lipstick."

Two days later she was sacked, ostensibly for bad work but it was really for something else.

"Did she swear?"

"No."

"What was it then?"

"I'm not repeating it."

"Go on, tell us. What did she say?"

"Ask Doris, she'll tell you."

Doris wouldn't say but Margaret agreed to whisper it at the tea break and afterwards we returned to our benches shocked into silence.

Mandy, apparently, while all the menders were open-mouthed, had regaled them with events of the previous Sunday afternoon with her boyfriend. This is what Mandy had said,

"As I lay on the bed he threw a glass of cold water over me and said, 'That should cool you down' ".

Sheila, the girl facing me along the bench had red hair that hung in waves down to her waist. She was tall, graceful and didn't know she was beautiful.

Sheila   "I don't want anything to do with boys they are horrible. All they want to know is whether I've got red hair down there."

Glancing up from her work, she said,

"By the way, in case you're wondering, the answer's 'Yes'."

Ann, nicely spoken and shy, had been married at sixteen to a Polish pilot named Yan, spelt with a J, and one year later he'd been killed in a training exercise.

Marion   "Imagine being married to a man named Yan spelt with a J. That's really romantic."

Me   "And to be killed a year later, that's even more romantic."

Marion   "Shall we ask her about it?"

Me   "About what?"

Marion   "You know, the wedding night, what it was like."

Me   "You ask her. Go on, now, while she's sitting down."

Jean   "Marion's asking her. She's cheeky."

We could see the two of them together at the far bench and we gathered round waiting for Marion's report. We knew what to do but not what it was like to do it. And here was somebody our age who could tell us.

Me   "She's been gone a long time."

Jean   "Ann won't tell her anything."

Me   "Shhh… Here she comes. What did Ann say?"

Marion   " 'Don't ask personal questions,' that's what she said."

Jean   "Told you."

Marion   "That's what she said first then she whispered something."

Me   "What did she whisper?"

Marion   "She said Yan was very gentle and very tender."

Jean   "Well, go on… "

Marion   "That's all she said honest, he was very gentle and very tender."

Jean   "That's real romance, that is."

French letters were a mystery; I had never seen one. One girl had a brother in the Navy who said French letters were supplied free to all the sailors. This was hard to believe because nobody would talk about such things to a brother.

Jane	"They sell French letters in Boots."
Sheila	"How do you know?"
Jane	"It says 'Durex sold here' "
Sheila	"They're not on the counter are they?"
Jane	"Course not. You have to ask for them. You have to say 'packet of three please.' "
Joyce	"You know Joan in the machine room?"
Me	"What about her?"
Joyce	"Her husband has to use a special one made of silk and he has to wash it out every time."
Me	"Why?"
Joyce	"Because the doctor says she mustn't have any more children."

On the first day back after her honeymoon, we stared at a cutter named Pat, looking for signs on her face. Pat's husband was an older man, short and serious and boring. Always in gauntlet gloves and motorbike gear, he had no interest in other girls and didn't even look at us. Pat had had TB and mother said TB made girls pretty.

Carefully avoiding the word 'honeymoon' I asked if she'd had a nice holiday.

Pat	"Yes thank you. The bike broke down on the way to Devon and we had to spend the first night at the side of the road on the grass verge."

We looked round at each other.

Ruth –	"Did you have love?"
Pat –	"Oh yes, we had love."

YHA

Mother	"You are not going and that's the end of it. If you think I'm letting you get into cars with strange men you've got another think coming young lady."
Me	"Why not?"
Mother	"Because I say so, that's why not."
Me	"Everybody does it."
Mother	"Not my daughter."
Me	"You let David go."
Mother	"That's different and you know it."
Me	"I never have adventure. Eileen has adventures. She's in the Girls' Venture Scouts, she goes."
Mother	"I'm not standing here arguing, the beds need making."

We were talking about youth hostelling. Youth hostels with their big triangular YHA signs were dotted all over the country, at least two were in Leicestershire, at Knossington and Copt Oak, but they were too near. Most hikers headed for the hills of Derbyshire and its eight hostels.

The idea behind YHA was to encourage young workers to leave the city at weekends and the organisation provided cheap accommodation to those travelling 'under their own steam', which meant walking or cycling. Overnight beds in a dormitory cost one shilling and sixpence (7.5p) and you could cook your own food. It sounded like a great way to meet boys.

My brother went to hostels with a knapsack packed with bacon in greaseproof paper and a tin of beans. With his friend he would start at Red Hill roundabout at Birstall ready to hike north.

Although this was a popular and exciting pastime, I was not interested until I saw a YHA badge on the green jumper of Eileen, a girl at work I admired. Eileen was different from other girls, she never gossiped or joined in the singing but I liked her because she seemed grown up and independent. As well as the Girls Venture Scouts she looked after a Brownie pack. Her fair hair was worn, not in curls like the rest of us, but short and straight.

I took her home for tea, knowing she'd be a pushover and after she'd gone mother said, "What a sensible girl, she looks wholesome and refined."

Me   "Well can I go hiking with her then?"

Mother   "I'll talk to your dad."

* * *

With strict instructions never to get into a vehicle with more than one man in we set off on the last Saturday of the year to Ilam Hall in Derbyshire because they were having a folk dancing party for the New Year.

The route was in four stages. Stage one as far as Loughborough, then a long walk to Hathern Road to hitch a lift to Derby and then on to the youth hostel.

After Derby we had not had a lift for about an hour when it began to snow; there were no weather forecasts then. Heads down under our hoods we trudged on in a blizzard that felt like sharp needles hitting my face. It was getting dark and traffic was thinning out when, at last, a van pulled up.

In the front seat I could just make out two men and a dog.

Me (in panic)   "No, no, Eileen, say 'No', there are two of them."

Eileen   "Come on, it's the only chance we'll get."

Man in van   "Where you making for?"

Eileen   "Ilam youth hostel."

Man in van   "Jump in the back then, we'll take you there."

"No, no!" I urged, tugging Eileen's coat as she made for the back of the van.

Eileen (over the engine noise)   "These men are OK, get in."

My hands were so cold I couldn't open the van door but it was opened from inside where there were two more men. "Come in lads," one of them said helping us up and shutting the door against the wind.

Man in back of van "Ee they're not lads, they're young ladies."

The two men were on wooden benches and we sat opposite with a sack between us on the floor; in the folds of the sack were four dead rabbits. While I sat trembling, from the cold and from worry in case mother found out, Eileen talked to the men about Leicester Tigers. I thought it was an army regiment. The wind banged against the sides as the van made its way through the blizzard.

Youth hostels were originally huge private houses and the oak panelled entrance hall was full of warmth and activity as we queued up to sign in at the warden's office. From somewhere came the smell of bacon frying and a great clatter of pans.

Eileen   "That'll be the members' kitchen where we cook dinner. We queue for frying pans, and we have to wash them for the next person before we eat so food's always cold."

Boys were running up and down the noisy staircase with its big curved bannister carrying boxes of games. Two boys were speaking French.

A list of rules on the wall said:

Indoor shoes to be worn at all times

No smoking

No dogs

No noise after 11 p.m.

Sunday 11 a..m. prayers in the reading room are voluntary

HOUSE DUTIES ARE COMPULSORY

I'd heard about house duties, how people had to do a cleaning job before they could leave in the mornings, jobs like washing floors and polishing the stairs and how everybody tried to get out of it.

The warden was handing over sleeping bags, made of white cotton sheeting with envelope tops to cover pillows. Then it was our turn to sign in.

Warden   "I hoped you've booked, we're full."

Eileen   "We're wayfarers."

Warden   "I'm sorry. We're full up."

Eileen   "Both dormitories?"

Warden   "Both dormitories."

Eileen   "Is the family room vacant?"

Warden   "All full."

Eileen   "But there are supposed to be beds kept for wayfarers."

Warden   "Wayfarers' beds went at 6 o'clock. It's New Year's Eve."

Handing over a slip of paper he said, "Here, Mrs Drayling, second cottage past the post office. She'll take you in. Come back for the party about nine thirty. Next please."

Out we went into the cold and the snow, tired and hungry

Me   "What if the cottage is full?"

Eileen   "We'll go back and sleep in the games room. He's not allowed to turn anybody away."

Eileen knew the rules.

That small bright room in the cottage was like heaven. A big fire, smelling of wood smoke and coal, blazed in a black cooking range under a mantelpiece weighed down with photographs, mostly soldiers. Mrs Grayling hung our wet scarves and gloves on a string over the fireplace.

Mrs Grayling	"Now what do you pay at the hostel?"
Eileen	"One and sixpence."
Mrs Grayling	"What about your supper?"
Eileen	"We've brought our own."
Mrs Grayling	"You can both sleep in this room, one on the sofa and one on the floor and I'll give you breakfast. You pay me two shillings each. And you can listen to *In Town Tonight* with us."

"Thank you very much", I said quickly, dreading the very idea, "but we're going to go to a folk dancing party at the hostel."

"Oh," said Mrs Grayling, "you'll have to be back before half-past eleven. That's when we go to bed, New Year or no New Year."

The fireside chairs and the sofa were covered with blankets and cushions, all colours and all hand knitted. Every time Mr Grayling tried to speak his wife interrupted so he didn't say much. In front of the fire was a rug made from strips of waste material pegged into a canvas backing, again all colours, and that's where Eileen and I sat frying our bacon and beans with two ginger cats that whacked each other all the time as they tried to pinch the bacon which we were eating from the pan.

When the wind blew outside the smoke flickered up the chimney. The room was so cosy with the crackle of the fire and the click of Mrs Grayling's knitting pins that I began to wish we weren't going out at all. I felt bad about it because Eileen had arranged the weekend but plucking up courage I whispered to her, "Do you mind if I don't come with you tonight?"

She said, "I wasn't going back anyway. I don't care for the warden."

* * *

While we listened to the Light Programme on the wireless Mrs Grayling brought in a tray with four glasses of parsnip wine and some slices of Bakewell pudding, a round cake with yellow paste in the middle. The wine didn't taste very nice but I drank it. Afterwards Mr Grayling banked up the fire with slack, put a plate outside with a piece of coal on it and some coins to bring luck in the New Year, then they went to bed.

A paraffin heater stood in a corner of the outside lavatory to stop the pipes from freezing up and squares of newspaper hung from a nail on the wall.

Snuggled under blankets, me on the sofa and Eileen on the floor we lay awake talking by the dwindling firelight and listening to the bells of Ilam church ringing in the New Year.

About five in the morning when I could sleep no more because the fire had gone out and I was cold, even if both cats were snuggling up to me, came a scraping noise from the front of the house. Eileen was nowhere to be seen.

The snow had stopped when I pushed the curtain aside, Eileen, fully dressed, was clearing a path with a spade. As I pushed it open the bottom frame of the window rested on top of a snowdrift.

Eileen   "Put some clothes on and fetch another spade from the shed."

Me   "Can't Mr Grayling do it?"

Eileen   "No, we need to set off early. Hurry up."

With snow up to our knees and with church bells ringing, we cleared a path, piling up the light fluffy snow on either side.

Me   "Why do we have to set off so early?"

Eileen   "Sunday is a bad day for lifts, no lorries and most of the cars have families in: they won't stop. In another hour the roads will be full of hikers from the hostel. We need to get going and make for the café at Ashbourne. People in the café might give us a lift to Derby."

Eileen knew everything.

"Happy New Year both of you." Mr Grayling was watching us from the front door in a long tweed coat over pyjamas. "Well you are good girls. Fancy saving me all that work. We'll not take any money from you both. Your breakfast's ready." It was the most we'd heard him say.

We sat on stools at a table in the scullery next to a shallow brown sink eating porridge and Derbyshire oatcakes.

Mrs Grayling wore a brown felt hat with a feather but she didn't eat anything because she was off to communion and had to go on an empty stomach. When she'd gone Eileen left two shillings on the mantelpiece and nodded to me to do the same.

We set off up a winding lane with little walls at the side partly hidden under snowdrifts. The world looked a different place from the night before because we were in the middle of a great silence of snow.

Spread out on all sides, near and in the distance, were white hills divided by winding stonewalls that looked as if somebody had drawn them.

Eileen seemed to like walking on ahead and I didn't mind because I was thinking about the next day at work and how to describe the adventure to the girls, of course I wouldn't mention the men in the van in case it got back to mother.

The first lift was in the front of a truck with milk churns in the back driven by a man who said he'd got up every morning at half-past three for twenty-two years.

I can't remember any more about the journey home.

I loved that cottage. And the cats.

MARSHA

Marsha was a vivacious girl with flashing eyes, thick black hair and a mischievous expression. She was a fast and skilful worker earning top wages and friendly with Nellie, who was her mentor, if mentors exist in hosiery factories. Nellie knitted two jumpers for Marsha, both the same, one to wear and one in the wash. I thought it strange to have two jumpers the same colour.

Joyce, calling across the room: "It's my wedding anniversary next week, three years."

Marsha   "Three years and no babies. I don't think your marriage has been consumed."

Nellie   "Marsha! That's not the word. It's not 'consumed', it's 'consominated'."

Marsha lived in a little back-to-back house. I went there once, into the bright front room with embroidered cloths and china cups. There were nine children in the family and every child had its own household job; the three-year-old was standing on a stool washing spoons. Eventually the eldest boy went to grammar school and became the dean of a cathedral.

With her trim figure and lively personality Marsha was never short of boyfriends. There was a Thursday man who took her to the theatre once a week, a Sunday afternoon man at a church club and several others queuing up for dates.

Mr Jenkins, the foreman at work, was a staid man in a white coat who gave out the work and checked time slips. He was not the type to flirt but from the way he lingered round her counter it was obvious he liked Marsha. One day we heard him ask her in an innocent and matter-of-fact way, "You know those black hairs on your leg, do they go all the way to the top?"

We looked round at each other, open-mouthed and wondering how Marsha would react. She laid down her cutting shears, marched round the counter and faced him squarely. Banging her fists onto her hips, she stood and glared at him with fury till he slunk away whimpering, "I'm sorry, I'm sorry, I'm sorry."

He was over forty; she was seventeen.

It was Marsha who ran the perm club for a local hairdresser. Every factory had, among its workforce, people who organised raffles, sweepstakes on horses and other enterprises. The perm club had eleven members willing to pay one pound a week for twelve weeks towards a perm that cost eleven pounds. Each week a name was drawn from a hat to see whose turn it was to get that week's perm. Marsha's reward was a free perm at week twelve, which, of course had been paid for by the other members.

MR CATTELL

New jobs were easy to find and workers often went from one factory to another, taking their friends with them. They knew which companies paid bonuses, which gave turkeys away at Christmas and which ones organised the best seaside outings in summer.

Friends in the drama group I belonged to worked in offices. Typists and invoice clerks needed a certificate from a commercial college and my family could not afford it but I decided to try for some kind of general office work even if the pay was not as good as cutting.

Among the advertisements in the *Mercury* were two jobs I fancied, one for a dress designer, the other for an office assistant. I applied, in writing, for both and found myself in a dress factory being interviewed by Mr Cattell, who was thin, pale and over six feet tall. He seemed to have trouble finding somewhere to arrange his long legs as he sat talking to me. All the time he was speaking, which he did beautifully, he stroked and twisted his long flying officer moustache. Whenever I hear the word 'gentleman' now I always think of Mr

*Mr Cattell sketched
by Ann Thornton.*

Cattell in his brown shoes and brown, three-piece pin-striped suit and the fruity woodland whiff of his pipe.

Behind the glass I could see, and hear and smell, the whole factory and all those girls sitting on stools crouched over machines.

Mr Cattell   "What are your qualifications, Miss Rogers?"

Me   "Qualifications?"

Mr Cattell   "Yes, your design qualifications."

Me   "Oh, I'm not qualified but I can draw dresses."

Mr Cattell   "I'm sure you're very good at drawing. Now tell me about your experience of knitwear design."

Me   "Well, I thought I could learn it here."

Mr Cattell   "Miss Rogers, I'm afraid designers need art college qualifications or at least two years experience with a high class firm."

When I said I didn't know about that he said, "I'm very sorry you have had a journey for nothing. Will you please allow me to reimburse your bus fares?"

Like I said, a gentleman.

The office job interview was a pushover so I gave a week's notice to the underwear factory and turned up the following Monday all dressed up in an office worker's outfit, tweed skirt and jacket, bought on hire purchase, and a white blouse.

They showed me how to operate a Gestetner duplicating machine, which involved fastening a stencil to a roller, pouring in methylated spirits and turning a handle. Interesting work, and fun for the first half hour, but there was a lot of day left after that and nobody spoke to me.

Next day came a letter from Mr Cattell asking me to call back to see him.

"I hope I have not brought you here on a fool's errand Miss Rogers," he said, offering me a chair. Having no idea what he meant I replied in a posh voice, "Not at all, Sir."

"There's something about you, something about you that… "

I waited, but instead of finishing the sentence, he told me there was a vacancy for a petton grader. I tried to look intelligent although I'd never heard of such a job. "Somebody to take a paper petton," (Ah! He meant a pattern.) "for a small size dress and re-cut it in larger sizes." If I wanted it I could have that job and I would be trained.

I didn't go back to the office job, ever. They still owe me a day's pay.

THE DRESS FACTORY

I. and L. Stevens occupied the ground floor of a two-storey building on Charles Street. The upper floor housed a cigar factory owned by the brother-in-law of Mr Cattell. I once peeked inside to see long benches covered in huge dry leaves and the atmosphere was cold and dead. The dress factory had about fifty workers and produced top quality dresses under various labels including Susan Small. These dresses were displayed in the windows of city centre shops at a price equivalent to three or four weeks' wages.

There was a cutting room, pressing room, machine room and packing room. Despite the name they were not rooms, merely different areas of the factory, which was all one floor and meant that my work area was much noisier than Arthur Foister's Cherub works. Along one side were big windows but lights still had to be on all day. The boss, Mr Cattell, had his office at one end of the factory divided from us by a glass screen.

On that first morning I watched, confused and anxious, as Helen, a cutter-grader, took me through a list of specifications for dress sizes. But I knew this

This becoming princess-line model by Susan Small makes a perfect garden party dress. In Rose-beige lace over matching net, it has its own stiffened taffeta foundation, and taffeta inserts run between the lace panels. Available from Bunton at approximately 24½ guineas.

An ideal Garden Party Dress

Susan Small dress advertised in Leicester Graphic in August 1955. The price is shown as 24½ guineas (£25.75).

At this time women's wages were about £6 a week so the dress represents over four weeks' wages.

work was for me having seen all the colourful dresses hanging near the machines in various stages of being made up. Helen, who was friendly and encouraging, introduced me to people I would be in contact with including the sample machinist and the forelady.

Long after other workers had come in I noticed three girls wafting importantly through the factory and disappearing into a glass partitioned room at the far end.

Me	"Who are they?"
Helen	"They are the designers."
Me	"Why do they come late?"
Helen	"Oh, designers don't keep factory hours."
Me	"Do they stay in that room?"
Helen	"Oh, no, they'll be in and out checking work, and they'll be checking your patterns."
Me	"I like their clothes."
Helen	"They go to fashion shows."
Me	"Fashion shows?"
Helen	"They're always going to London shows and once a year they go to Ascot races. Julie's just married an architect, he sometimes comes in."
Me	"Comes in the factory?"
Helen	"Of course, and the boyfriends of the other two, both artists, they come in."

The only men working in the factory, apart from the caretaker and mechanic, were the packers who folded finished garments into boxes and labelled them ready for the van, which came weekly to transport garments to London. Also on the van but travelling on a dress rail, were new designs to be approved by head office.

The mechanic looked after the machinery if it broke down and he was always busy. Lockstitch machines joined two seams together just like ordinary domestic sewing machines. Overlock machines joined two seams in a way that allowed the fabric to stretch, otherwise the stitching on knitted fabric would break when the garment was pulled on. Overlocking also trimmed off excess fabric as it sewed the seam. Quality knitted dresses had both lockstitch and overlocked seams. Three reels of cotton were needed on an overlocker and three needles had to be threaded. As soon as the operative pressed the foot pedal the cottons came whizzing off the spindles making a dash for the needles. Almost every tee-shirt and sweater today is made on these machines, an amazing invention. Overlockers worked at great speed and earned more than other workers except cutters.

A pin tuck machine picked up a tiny ridge of fabric and sewed it through from side to side creating a raised pattern on a yoke. A hemmer made a stitch at the bottom of a garment that was loose enough not to show through on the outside. All this machinery had to be kept in good order and, as well as the factory mechanic, Mike Harper from the Singer Sewing Machine Company was often called in. A girl's wages depended on piecework (irrespective of age they were called 'girls') and if the machine broke down they were idle and lost money.

THE DESIGN OFFICE

The best thing about 'petton' grading was the position of the worktable, just outside the design office, from where I could see and hear much of what went on. Sometimes in the mornings, before the designers arrived, I would go in and touch things especially the buttons. These button samples were on showcards. There were buttons of all shapes, buttons of glass and pearl, buttons of leather and buttons as big as biscuits. There were lace collars to feel and rolls of linen to smell. Dressmakers' dummies were used for creating patterns by draping muslin straight on to a body and once, when a dress was half pinned onto a dummy, I added some extra gathers.

The glass partition separating the room from the factory was covered in full-page advertisements for day dresses and evening gowns, torn out from French magazines, and they were reflected in the huge wall mirror opposite. Each one of these black and white pictures was a work of the photographer's art and now regarded as classic images. Models struck a superior pose, in the sculpted styling and sumptuous fabrics, over signatures of the great names of Paris fashion houses, Balanciaga, Chanel, Hermes and Schiaparelli. These pictures, from French *Vogue* and *L'Officiel,* the standard records of couture, were replaced from time to time with any new ones that caught the eye of I. and L. Stevens' designers.

From my worktable outside I could often hear the designers talking. Everything French was good: French singers, French cloth, French cheese. Rachel King, the head designer, had been to Mr Cattell's holiday house at somewhere called Le Lavendue in France . They talked of French films they'd seen at the Floral Hall. But only black and white and only with sub-titles. Coloured films were 'so vile' and dubbing was one of the many things they sneered at along with the *Daily Mirror*, tinned soup and people who said 'brassiere' instead of 'bra.'

They read books called *Brideshead* and *Vile Bodies* by Evelyn Waugh who turned out to be a man, and writers called Dostoyevsky, Tolstoy, Proust and Zola. I borrowed these books from the library the minute they were mentioned and none of them were hard to read except Proust, I couldn't see anything in him. The woman at the library had trouble finding a book called *Mennertarms*; she said, "Do you mean *Men at Arms?*"

One Monday morning they were full of talk about Diagalev, some stage designer, whose ballet they'd been to see in London. That was the 'bees' knees'. Anything good was always 'the bees' knees'. There was a picture of a Russian ballerina on display among the fashion pictures on the wall. She was leaning against a door and wearing a frumpy sweater. Underneath it said 'even age and crumpled tights cannot spoil the poetry of her legs.'

Apart from the occasions when a pattern piece needed checking, these girls, with tape measures permanently dangling round their necks, hardly noticed me at my worktable. Rachel was of small stature with straw-coloured hair and boyish good looks. Her features were flattish but she was amazingly attractive with a haughty expression as she pressed her fingers onto the pattern paper to show me how to shape an armhole or a neckline. When she stood that close her perfume smelt expensive and luxurious. The clothes she wore were plain and classic and of a quality I had never seen in a shop. Black French sweater, thin silk Jaeger scarf, tweed A-line skirt that tilted from side to side as she walked, and kitten-heeled shoes. The bees' knees.

SATURDAY NIGHTS

The purpose of work was to earn enough to go out dressed up on Saturdays. All week long we looked forward to Saturday nights and the possibility of some excitement.

Morning was spent in town at Brucciani's cream and green, spacious café in Horsefair Street, queuing up to be served by Mr B himself. "Hurry along please. No more than six at one table. Hurry along *please*."

All the smart youth of Leicester met there to talk and smoke and flirt at the round tables that could easily take a dozen of us. The shining ones from the art college had their own tables and we tried not to let them see us looking in their direction but they were too involved with each other ever to glance at us. The minute our cups were empty Mr B would clear the tables so the trick was always to have some coffee left in the cup.

Saturday afternoons were for getting ready, perhaps making a dress or trying out new make-up and hairdos.

The Palais de Danse in Humberstone Gate was a wonderful dance hall with its two bands one above the other, a fountain in the middle of the floor, twirling mirror ball and a balcony where a boy might invite you for coffee. But you had to think hard before accepting because you could be stuck with him all evening, the evening that began in the ladies cloakroom changing outdoor footwear into gold or silver dance shoes brought from home in a brown paper bag. A good ten minutes in front of the mirror then downstairs to stand at the side trying not to look hopeful but longing to hear, "Can I have this dance please?"

It was not polite to refuse except if they were old or smelling of garlic; some foreigners never stood a chance. To avoid an unwelcome partner you had to look away when you saw him coming, that always put them off. If you were left without a partner there were strategies for saving face. Animated chatting to a friend with back turned to the dance floor or enthusiastic waves to imaginary people up in the balcony.

The bandsmen were old but the beat was infectious. Foxtrots, quick steps, waltzes and ladies 'excuse-me' quick steps where you tapped a man on the shoulder and he had to relinquish his partner and dance with you. A good looker could find himself with many different partners in the ladies 'excuse-me'. Of course nobody said they worked in a factory. That would be unthinkable. If somebody asked where you worked you made something up, "office work," "air hostess," "management trainee." The word "factory" was out.

Jiving was the rage and some were terrific at it, especially little men, who could dance leaning backwards almost parallel with the floor and with one arm waving for balance they swung their partner so high you glimpsed her knickers. The floor cleared for a good jiving couple. Men wore long jackets called drapes and crepe-soled shoes nicknamed 'brothel creepers'. Girls wore full skirts with stiff petticoats, sometimes two or three together, and they were meant to show.

The art school crowd sometimes came to the Palais but much later in the evening and they hadn't spent all afternoon getting ready; they wore the same clothes they wore for work, but still looked terrific. One quick dance with each other and they disappeared, probably to some party in the country to discuss Proust.

If you struck lucky by the end of the evening you might have found somebody interesting and, "Can I walk you home?" was the next stage. While we queued on the stairs to collect coats and shoes the boys stood outside waiting for us, nobody had a car then. Their reward for walking us home was a quick kiss at the front gate where my dad always happened to be putting out the milk bottles just as I arrived. After the kiss the invitation, "Can I see you again?" We said 'Yes' and then didn't turn up if we weren't keen.

Sunday night under Kemps clock (now above Starbucks) at seven was a typical meeting place. Of course the girl was never there first; we hid round the corner till we saw the boy, waited a few minutes, then ran up and apologised for being late. As my mother said, "You must always let the boys think they are doing the chasing."

The Odeon and the Savoy were popular cinemas for Sunday evening dates and the boy paid for the tickets. Girls offered to pay of course, in a half-hearted way, and sometimes bought the chocolates. On a Sunday in summer the meeting place might be St Margaret's Bus Station for the bus to Bradgate Park where boys hoping for a snog in the bracken carried a raincoat.

CHRISTMAS IN THE FACTORY

Christmas came early to the dress factory. From October onwards women put deposits on toys for their children; and deposits were lost if the rest of the money was not paid off within two months. These were expensive toys, bikes or pedal cars for boys, dolls and prams for girls. Some deposits were even put down on winter coats.

Me   "Why do shops keep deposits and give you nothing?"

My dad   "Workers are always robbed. Except in Russia."

In mid-December a letterbox, fashioned from cardboard and red crepe paper, was placed in the middle of the factory and all our Christmas cards to each other were posted in it. Then came trimming up day when windows were criss-crossed with twisted bands of coloured paper and every dress rail and girder was festooned with lammetta, a type of tinsel. The dinner hour that day was bustling with activity; instead of going home we ate sandwiches.

Presents to each other were not surprises but the result of much excited bargaining over the weeks.

"You give me this, I'll give you that."

"Here it is," my friend announced, rushing in from the shops with a brown paper bag in her hand. Inside was something I'd looked forward to for weeks. A lipstick, not any lipstick, but a Max Factor lipstick. Max Factor, the make up of the stars.

Although this was years after the war, luxury goods were only just coming in and there were queues at Lewis's department store when Max Factor consignments arrived. It was very expensive and special customers could reserve something.

LEWIS'S
FASHION PARADES

It's Spring again—time to buy something new! Lewis's cordially invite you to the Spring Fashion Parades to be held on the Fashion Floor (Second Floor) to see all that's new in fashions. Tickets are obtainable from the Travel Bureau (First Floor) or on any of the Fashion Departments.

Tuesday, 12th March
1 p.m., 3 p.m.

Wednesday, 13th March,
11 a.m., 3 p.m., 5.30 p.m.

Friday, 15th March
12.30 p.m., 3 p.m.

LEWIS'S (MIDLAND) LTD., HUMBERSTONE GATE, LEICESTER Telephone 23241

Lewis's department store Humberstone Gate from an advert in the March 1957 issue of the Leicester Graphic.

Max Factor's wonderful glamorous lipstick
Copyright The Procter & Gamble Company.

"Only one item per customer please," announced the Lewis's girls dolled up in white coats and plucked eyebrows, "one lipstick or one refill but not both."

And here was mine at last. To feel the weight of the gold case with its embossed pattern of tiny squares was to embrace that far off world of luxury and glamour beyond dreams. To remove the top and twist the base till the shiny red cylinder emerged with a scent of sweet vanilla was to experience the world of open top cars with white steering wheels, driven by handsome men in white suits and shining partings leaning forward to light cigarettes for beautiful women with perfect hair and perfect teeth beneath skies that were ever blue.

Coral Tone was the lipstick colour and just to say the name made me feel beautiful.

On the last afternoon before the three-day holiday, machines were switched off, two girls emptied the letterbox and delivered the cards round the room while trestle tables, covered in red crepe paper with scallops cut along the edge, displayed mince pies, sausage rolls and Walkers pork pies. Mr Cattell provided lemonade, beer and sherry. But not wine, wine was something only French people drank.

Afterwards, Mr Cattell passed cigars to the men and the place smelt lovely and Christmassy. While the office people stood at one end of the factory and the shining ones at the other, Mrs Bennett with her white thin face stood near the ironing boards and sang in a high-pitched voice,

"Trumpeter, what are you sounding now, is it the call I'm seeking."

Then she sang some more verses, then something about treading light o'er the dead in the valley, then a few more verses. When she finished with, "Till the trumpeter sounds the last rally," a woman removed Mrs Bennett's glasses for her and wiped her eyes. I whispered to my friend, "Why is she crying?"

"Because her son went down with the Ark Royal."

"What's the Ark Royal?"

"Some ship."

After tapping on a girder with a teaspoon Mr Cattell, with his beautiful upper class stammer, made a speech. First he thanked Mrs Bennett for her singing and said it was a fine thing to remember the boys who had given their lives for us in the war. Then he thanked all of us for our hard work in a difficult year, and asked us to convey his compliments of the season to our families and we could all go home an hour earlier. Somebody shouted, "Three cheers for Mr Cattell," and we did "Hip-hip, hurray!"

After that everybody sang together, "We wish you a Merry Christmas, " before hurrying out to join the crowds in Leicester market carrying last minute presents and buying turkeys.

THE DAFFODIL CARDIGAN

One afternoon I found, under the back of the counter behind a pipe, a dirty garment that had obviously been there for some time. Covered with dust, threads and fluff it appeared at first to be a greyish colour but the inside, unfolded was yellow and then I saw it. A blue label with the embroidered signature, 'Elsa Schiaparelli'. I had found a Paris couture cardigan.

From time to time head office in London purchased, at considerable cost, a couture garment from France with the sole purpose of sending it to Leicester to copy, not the design, but the underlying shape. Each manufacturer worked from their own basic pattern, known as 'the block.' and from this block every pattern was developed. But, because fashion silhouettes change in many subtle ways, the block needed regular updating with a new French pattern.

The cardigan under my counter was one of these special purchases, which should have been sent back to London, but it had been overlooked.

At first I kept it hidden but nobody came looking for it. In the end, I showed it to Mr Cattell and asked if I could borrow it for the weekend.

"What, this dirty thing?" he said, and I pointed to the Schiaparelli label.

"Ah, well, that's entirely a different matter," he said, holding it out at arm's length and making sucking noises while he pondered. Passing it back he whispered, "Take it home and keep it," adding, with a twinkle in his eye, "best not to wear it for work."

I loved Mr Cattell and wished he could be my father.

In the wash it came up a beautiful daffodil yellow. Knitted from mercerised cotton, a yarn that is twisted and polished after spinning to produce a sheen, the design was so simple that in the street nobody would have looked at it twice, but it was a perfect classic, short sleeved, summer cardigan. There were no seams anywhere because the welt, sleeves and stole were knitted into the shape. Nine mother-of-pearl buttons with rubber shanks for comfort formed the front fastening with hand-made buttonholes for strength.

The fit was superb, sitting so lightly on the waist and shoulders you hardly knew you were wearing it at all. Like all quality garments it bestowed elegance and poise on the wearer. Such is the effect of couture.

Every autumn the cardigan was put away in tissue paper till summer came round again and by the time it showed any sign of wear I had grown up children. Such is the economic value of couture.

MY BIG BREAK

I had been grading patterns into different sizes for about two months when, one Friday morning, Mr Cattell, on his way round the factory, asked how I was getting on. He wanted to know if the work was interesting and if there was enough space. I told him I liked the job but some of the designs were too plain at the back. He stopped and asked what I meant.

"This one, for example," I explained, pointing to a blue woollen dress on its hanger.

Mr Cattell	"What's wrong with it?"
Me	"The back bodice has no feature."
Mr Cattell	"Does that matter?"
Me	"It does if the fabric is plain."
Mr Cattell	"A woman can't see the back of a dress in a shop window."
Me	"She can when she tries it on."
Mr Cattell	"Really?"
Me	"Yes, we twist round."
Mr Cattell	"Come with me to see Miss King."

It was nearly dinnertime when the two of us stepped into the design office where the designers were putting coats on and preparing to leave.

"Do excuse us butting in Miss King, but Mary would like to try her hand at a design."

Rachel, picking up her handbag, said in a dismissive manner, "Oh anyone can design, can she cut a pattern?"

I felt silly because I couldn't; making an original pattern was a special skill.

"Of course she can't," Mr Cattell answered in his polite way, "but I'm sure you will help her with it," and out the three of them went.

"Choose a fabric this afternoon," he said, with an encouraging tap on my shoulder, "and see what you can do." Then he left the room as well.

I was alone, feeling foolish and wishing I'd not said a word about the designs.

Instead of going home I went to Woolworths and bought a writing pad without lines and a yellow pencil with a rubber at the end.

* * *

Fabrics were stored in the factory basement, a place that in summer was always cold and in winter was full of fumes from the boiler. As soon as the afternoon shift began I went down to look through the new rolls of cloth with their swinging tickets and names of local firms such as Shipley Jayes and Jerseycraft. These fabrics, with their comforting smell of new wool, were knitted on machines made in Leicester by companies like Mellor Bromley, Stibbe and Wildt. Local dye works coloured the yarns that had been spun nearby. Some of the wool would have come from a breed of sheep called Border Leicesters that grazed the wet green pastures of the eastern county. Leicestershire grass is so rich that farmers in the north of England used to rent the fields for grazing their stock.

I chose a honey-beige cloth and self-consciously walked through the factory behind the caretaker who carried the roll over his shoulder to my table. Sitting on a high stool I set about drawing collars and cuffs on the Woolworths pad, aware that other workers were watching. They were hard at work on machining, I was sketching.

After a while Rachel King came and stood looking over my shoulder, so close I could feel the fabric of her new skirt against my arm. Without saying a word and with a swish of her pleats she hurried away.

It was hard fighting the tears as I stared at my pathetic sketch, then came the slam of a magazine on the table. It was Rachel with French *Vogue* and a roll of paper.

"Put your drawings away," she said, "flick through this magazine very quickly. Then go through again page by page looking only at silhouettes and skirt length, nothing else. Spend at least an hour doing that. Then close it up and put it away. You will then be ready to draw. This is cartridge paper. Use it. If I can spare the time on Monday you can show me your ideas."

* * *

In the history of the fashion industry few dresses could have had so much time spent on the first sketch. The weekend was given over to rubbing out and starting again; the whole family had a go at it.

On Monday, between two pieces of cardboard, the drawing was taken to work. I worried because it was raining and I was afraid the cardboard would get wet. On top of it all the bus was held up because the conductor pressed the bell too soon and an old lady missed her footing as she stepped on. Busses did not have doors at that time. She had hurt her knee and I moved up to make room for her, immediately regretting it because the cardboard was a bit crushed.

All day I graded patterns and waited for a chance to show Rachel what I'd done but there never seemed to be a suitable time to interrupt her comings and goings and by the middle of the afternoon I was desperate. I hadn't even dared to take a tea break in case I missed her. It was almost time to go home when I stood outside her door with French *Vogue* in one hand and the sketch in the other waiting for her to come out.

Me   "Excuse me Rachel, I've finished with this magazine."

Rachel   "Put it in the office will you?"

Me   "I wonder if you have time to look at my work?"

She looked surprised.

Rachel   "Oh, I'd forgotten about that. You'd better bring it in."

THAT FIRST PATTERN

Watching an expert at work, the speed, the precision, the balletic movements of the body, and the seemingly casual and effortless approach to a complicated task, is an exhilarating experience.

To make the pattern for my design Rachel King began by pinning the sketch to the wall and sweeping the counter clear with a swish of her yardstick. Standing next to the roll of brown paper that stood in the corner like a tree trunk she uncoiled a section, slicing it free from the roll with a downward cut of her shears, a procedure requiring caution because paper can cut flesh deeper than a knife. After reverse rolling the paper to make it lie flat she spread it on the table, placing weights on the four corners. Next she lifted the block pattern from its wall hook and laid it on the paper, drawing round it and adding, with a flick of the ruler, front facings and seam allowances. I stood watching her draw, freehand, the curve of an armhole, hardly daring to breath in the concentrated atmosphere of the situation and dreading anyone coming in to interrupt.

She glanced up at the sketch, "Collar width?" she asked, tape measure at the ready and starting a quick fire dialogue.

Me   "Four and a quarter inches."

Rachel   "Cuff width?"

Me   "The same."

Rachel   "Why?"

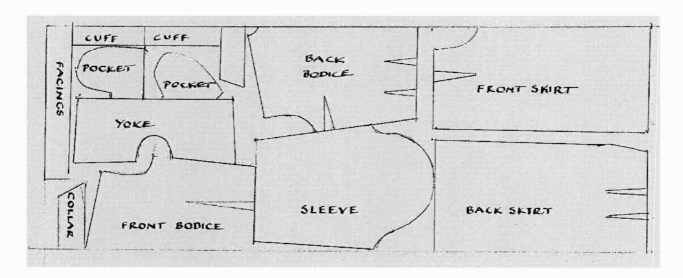

The layout for cutting the beige dress.

Me	"To match the collar."
Rachel	"Wrong. The eye deceives. For collar and cuff to look the same the cuffs must be cut narrower."

Then she asked how deep I wanted the back bodice yoke.

Me	"Five inches."
Rachel	"How will you get movement?"
Me	"Centre box pleat."
Rachel	"Impossible. The seam will be too thick."

Something inside sank. The back bodice was supposed to be cut like a man's shirt with a traditional pleat for movement and now she was saying it was not possible.

Me	"But there must be movement, what can I do?"
Rachel	"Ease it into the yoke. The machinist can push it under the machine foot, almost, but not quite, like gathering."

I nodded, and along the seam she wrote 'ease', before writing instructions on all the other pattern pieces marking the grain of the fabric with an arrow, 'Cut to fold', 'Cut four', 'Cut linings extra'.

With the pencil lying almost horizontal to the paper she drew a curved side seam to the skirt and I wondered why it wasn't drawn straight with the yardstick. Mind reading, she said, without even glancing up, "There are no straight lines on the human body."

The pattern was now finished and on the front skirt she wrote instructions for trimmings, 'Belt, buttons, tapes, linings.'

After swishing the waste paper off the table into the bin Rachel began to arrange the pieces to see how much fabric the dress would take, juggling big pieces this way and that, then fitting smaller pieces round them to make as little waste as possible.

"Let's call it one and three-quarter yards," she said, writing it down. "I'll leave you to draw a diagram of this layout. I'm away tomorrow, cut it out and if you make a mistake cut it again, never mind the cost, cost is irrelevant at this stage. Take it to my sample machinist and sit with her while she puts it together. "

Then she said something so amazing I thought I'd misheard.

"Be careful how you deal with her, a good machinist can make or mar your career."

This woman, the city's top designer, whom I worshipped and feared, had spoken of my job as a career.

THEY LIKED THE DRESS

Workers in factories knew everything that was going on. Nobody told them anything and no meetings were called but nothing was secret for long.

Even before they'd seen me sitting with Rachel's sample machinist they knew about my design as it progressed through the factory for lockstitching, contrast topstitching, overlocking, hemming, buttonholes and finishing. Some of the girls were resentful because workers do not push themselves forward, but others, especially older women, were interested and encouraging. A cutter, scuttling up to my table whispered, "Can Mavis do your buttons?"

Me	"No, no, Mavis is a presser."
Cutter (with a wink)	"Mavis does them better."
Me	"OK. Ask Mavis to do them."
Cutter	"Oh, no, it's not my place to ask her. You've got to do it."

Finally the dress was finished, looking good and hanging on the rail with other new designs. The honey beige garment was designed in a classic style, darted to the waist, long sleeves with cuffs and a straight skirt with a zipped side. The main feature was contrast topstitching round the cuffs and neckband in chocolate brown. This stitching was labour intensive requiring twenty rows one-eighth of an inch apart. What began as a sketch was now ready for wheeling out to the van bound for head office in London.

A few days later factory gossip said Rachel and Mr Cattell were talking about me in his office. What could I have done wrong?

Before long Mr Cattell's secretary, an alarmingly efficient woman in grey, marched the length of the factory to stand behind me and announce in that superior tone unique to boss's secretaries, "Mr Cattell would like to see you in his office."

The dress redrawn by Terri Bradshaw.

As usual the room smelt of pipe smoke. "Come in, come in," he said, indicating a seat near to Rachel. He was sitting in a leather swivel chair with a wooden rail round, his pipe resting on an ashtray next to a photo of his two boys outside their boarding school. Picking up a paper from the desk he pushed backwards with his long legs; somebody said he used to be a Spitfire pilot but he would never have fitted into the cockpit.

"I'll come straight to the point Mary, this memo has come from head office and I will read it to you, 'We note that one of the new designs submitted is by a Miss Rogers. We do not know who Miss Rogers is but we are most impressed with the design.' He waited for my reaction before saying, "Now what do you think of that?"

I didn't know what I was supposed to say. These were the two top people in the factory. I was used to speaking to them but one at a time, not both together and now I was being asked for my opinion on something.

"Of course," said Rachel, "it's because it's new. Anything by a new designer always attracts."

"Of course," I said, ever eager to agree with her and grateful at least for something to say.

Referring to her, as usual, in the third person, Mr Cattell said, "What would you think about working as Miss King's assistant?"

"Assistant?" I muttered.

He explained that the job entailed helping her in any way that was required; Miss King would supervise my design work when she had time and he would arrange for me to spend one day a week at the art college. He added that there would be a small cut in my wages because he would need to engage a new pattern grader in my place.

"Your full title will be junior assistant designer."

It was hard to take it in because all I wanted was to be alone and to repeat over and over in my head what the wonderful people at head office had said about my dress, "…we are most impressed with the design."

MY NEW CAREER

Next morning a space was found for me in the design room and my new job began. This included nipping to the market to buy oranges for Rachel, watering Rachel's cyclamen and carrying things out to Rachel's car which stood on Charles Street; car parks were not invented then.

"I don't keep a dog and bark myself," Rachel would joke from time to time adding that apprentices in Paris spend the first two years picking up pins from the floor.

That embarrassing cup.

Then there was the business of cups.

"Buy yourself a cup," she said, "then you can have tea with us instead of in the factory."

In Woolworths I bought a beautiful cup and saucer in yellow. On one side of the cup was a relief pattern of a thatched cottage with hollyhocks round the door.

Unwrapping it in the office, I placed it proudly on the tea tray and the three of them burst into fits of laughter.

"It's hideous," they shrieked while I stood there feeling small and silly. Their cups were by somebody called Suzie Cooper, blue with brown raised spots; I didn't know cups had to be designed. I couldn't understand why mine was hideous and discovered it was to do with something called good taste.

Mother   "Never mind good taste, a cup with a cottage sticking out one side is good fun."

Me   "Rachel says good taste has to be acquired."

Mother   "Tell her some are born with it."

There were other problems. It was difficult to know what to do when visitors came. For example when Monsieur Berthiez came with his samples of French buttons the three girls gathered round but I carried on working. Sometimes Rachel would say, "Do you want to come and look at these Mary?" and when that happened I never knew how long I was supposed to stand there.

Once when I spoke of 'my table' she said, "This is not your table. You are working on a corner of mine." Another time she took the hot spoon from her teacup and laid it on my bare arm; when I cried out with pain she laughed.

Tearfully I told one of the older women in the factory what Rachel had done.

Gladys   "She can be very spiteful."

Me   "But what shall I do?"

Gladys   "Put up with it, learn what you can."

Me   "Why is she so horrible to me?"

Gladys   "It's not just you. She's spoilt. She was an only child with no brothers and sisters to give her a good hiding when she needed one."

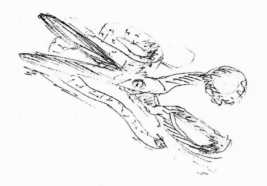

The very idea of anyone giving Rachel a good hiding was impossible to imagine. I learned not to stand nearby when she stirred her tea and discovered that the other two designers also had to keep out of her way at teatime.

But this was a new and exciting world and I could borrow clothes for going out in the evenings. It was part of a designer's job to wear dresses from the sample rail in order to try them out. What happens to a neckline, for instance, when the wearer leans forward or twists round? Will the sleeve still feel comfortable with the natural movement of the arm and will the dress hang well after sitting in it for a few hours? Is there enough room in a pencil skirt for striding along the street or climbing stairs. Of course a borrowed garment had to be returned to the rail next morning ready for any machinist who needed to see how it was put together.

Another good thing was listening to Rachel talking to the three of us about fashion. She said there was a fashion in everything, the way you hold a cigarette, the names you give your children, the food you eat for breakfast. She said fashion was the living pulse of the world and designers had to be aware of it by mixing with creative people and going to art shows. Reading a good newspaper was essential because it shaped our taste. Going regularly to London was also important. Pointing to some pink fabric, she said, "Money is irrelevant to good taste. Pink always looks cheap. That cinnamon colour there always looks expensive. They cost the same. Train your eye."

LONDON

The chance to go to London soon followed.

There were only half-a-dozen people on the cold bus at six o'clock that dark November morning and they were different from the people on my usual bus. One of them was a coal miner with a lamp on his helmet and when he got off he smiled at everybody, including me. How could somebody smile with such an awful job? The other passengers would be regulars who knew each other and I must have looked strange all dressed up at that time of the morning in a gold duster coat and black velvet hat.

I was off to head office in London with Rachel and a designer named Teresa; my job was to carry a parcel of dresses and Teresa was going to meet the London staff.

Rachel greeted me, shouting above the scream of an engine, "That's a ridiculous colour for a train journey."

Strolling backwards and forwards on the grimy platform at Leicester station, where the buffet windows still showed signs of wartime sticky tape, were people in the trade nodding to each other; men with briefcases and boxes of samples. Rachel chatted with another designer; they always stood out. Further along the platform was the usual sailor and, nearby, two of my brother's friends in National Service uniform smoking on a bench. But I pretended I didn't know them. Across the line was the Skegness platform where, in summer, queues of excited families struggled with enormous suitcases, quite different from today's London crowd.

Teresa, who was supposed to meet us at the station, had not turned up and I was alarmed to be told she wasn't coming; that meant I'd be alone all day with Rachel. What would I talk about? What could I say that would not feel silly?

There was the smell of soot and I was worried in case engine dirt was spoiling my coat, and my new suede court shoes were starting to pinch.

But this was like being on holiday and it seemed unreal to be sitting in a compartment for eight rattling along to London, watching fields whizzing by in the gathering light, while my friends were in the factory working. And it was paid for, and Mr Cattell, with his usual kindness, had taken me on one side and given me the money in advance.

'For your throat's sake smoke Craven A', 'Maxwell House coffee, worth waiting for', announced the makeshift hoardings hiding bomb sites as we approached St Pancras station where taxis were lined up on the platforms. One taxi driver helped a businessman off the train and carried his briefcase for him.

Leicester Square, Marble Arch, Piccadilly, Covent Garden. Reading these famous names on the Underground wall was like being in the middle of the world but Rachel didn't even have to stop to read the way. With a rumbling swoosh trains burst from the tunnel and people entered them as casually as their own back doors to sit staring straight ahead looking bored. How could people be bored on the Underground train in London?

The West End Headquarters of I. and L. Stevens had a boardroom for directors and a pink-carpeted showroom where I put down my parcel of dresses. When we entered the warm bustling machine room people greeted Rachel and I was amazed to hear the London accents. Just two hours away and people spoke differently.

Opposite: Off to London by train in my new gold coat with black hat and shoes.

Even before we took our coats off somebody said, "Miss Draycott wants to see you immediately," and Rachel looked worried.

I followed her to a small workroom where a woman with her back to us was draping muslin. She wore a check wool dress, too long, with clumpy shoes. The model, a picture of boredom, was facing us and I had to look away because under the muslin her bare nipples could clearly be seen. Without turning round and with no greeting, the older woman, waving an arm in the direction of a dress hanging on the wall opposite, said in a strange voice, "Darts off centre, skirt off balance, see to it." Taking the model by the arm she left the room and it was then I saw her dreadful face and was shocked. One side was stretched and twisted making one eye lower than the other and the mouth was pulled to one side, which would have accounted for the strange voice.

Taking her coat off Rachel examined the dress.

Rachel	"Another Teresa disaster."
Me	"What's wrong?"
Rachel	"A major pattern error."
Me	"It's not your fault. It's a mistake."
Rachel	"A designer is paid not to make mistakes. And in any case I am responsible for all the Leicester styling. Pass me those scissors."

Unpicking is a laborious task where every stitch is removed carefully until the pieces separate. But Rachel snipped through the first stitch, put down the scissors, grabbed the two sides of the skirt and ripped the expensive material apart in one movement with a loud crack. Turning to me she said, "Don't ever let me see you do that. Follow me, we deserve coffee".

Over coffee Rachel explained that Miss Draycott had been injured as a child in a fire. She was a Paris-trained *directrice*, and everybody was afraid of her, including the bosses, but she ran the firm with an iron hand. I kept thinking about the model.

Me	"I don't think the model was wearing anything under the muslin."

Rachel   "She was wearing talcum powder."

It was the first time Rachel had ever joked with me and I was pleased.

Carrying on a conversation as we hurried along Oxford Street was difficult, not only was it hard to speak over the traffic noise, but it seemed that each time I admired something in a window she was likely to say, "It's awful". Some windows displayed a photograph of the new young queen who would be crowned in a few months time. My feet were hurting but it was exciting to be among so many people in their best clothes and makeup hurrying along on a working day. People were actually wearing the sort of outfits that were normally only seen in magazines.

Bourne and Hollingsworth's department store was heaps better than any Leicester shop and I would have liked to wander on my own but Rachel was heading for Liberty's in Regent Street where she had a friend. A man wearing a top hat and a green uniform greeted us at the entrance of the beautiful galleried building, which was more like a stately home than a shop.

Rachel introduced me to her friend as 'my assistant' and while they chatted on the scarf counter I was sent down to the basement to look at a fabric called 'cotton lawn', a cloth as crisp and delicate as the flowers printed on it and it wore for years.

By the time I came back Rachel had bought three scarves.

"Pay more for a scarf than a dress", she said, "because a scarf lasts a lifetime but a dress goes out of fashion. These are silk, a silk scarf holds colour and never fades."

Once Rachel started talking fashion she couldn't stop and as I trailed after her round the store she was talking over her shoulder,

"Everything can be made a bit cheaper and a bit worse."

"Wear the colour of your eyes in the daytime and the colour of your hair at night."

"A black jumper always looks smart and with a different scarf and jewellery can look new every day."

Back in the chilly darkness of Leicester as we climbed the station steps she said, "You needn't rush to work in the morning, ten o'clock will do, and start sketching some of the London trends."

When I confessed I hadn't been looking out for them she said, "It's not what you see, it's what you absorb without knowing it, and next time you come to London don't wear new shoes."

* * *

Out of the blue came a solicitor's letter asking me to be a witness for the lady who fell off the bus. I had no idea how she knew my name and address. Mr Cattell gave me the day off and I wore a brown hat with a brim like witnesses wore in films.

Mother   "On your way buy some daffodils for the lady and when you give them to her wish her all the best for the case."

The woman and her husband were waiting for me with the solicitor who said I must not discuss my evidence.

Husband   "Oh, look she's brought us half a dozen daffs, that is kind."

I was cross. It's funny how words can change something nice to something ordinary. 'Half a dozen daffs' made the spring flowers sound cheap.

Afterwards a clerk asked what my daily wage was and when I said I was paid weekly he worked something out, passed me the money and gave me a paper to sign.

Dad   "You can only accept money if you've lost wages you silly girl."

Me   "What shall I do?"

Dad   "You must give it Mr Cattell."

Mr Cattell told me to keep it. Dad said if only all bosses were like that there would be no need for trade unions.

ASCOT

Creative people need to move in creative circles and London designers were sent to Paris. Leicester staff went to London fashion shows and, once a year, in June, I. and L. Stevens sent its team to Ascot races. With much excitement the three designers talked of little else except their Ascot outfits and I was, of course, extremely interested in their plans. A fitted coat of grey silk, cut from a Givenchy pattern, was being made in the workroom for Rachel. Linda said if you wore good shoes and carried a good bag the dress didn't matter at all. Teresa said she would borrow her aunt's crocodile bag but Teresa couldn't speak the truth by accident so nobody believed her. Long, thin umbrellas were the rage, more for posing than rain, and they were making umbrella covers to match their clothes. These were cut diagonally across the fabric like a man's tie; in fact, a man's tie was perfect for an umbrella cover once the narrow end was snipped off.

One afternoon while all this talk was going on, I was passing pins to Rachel who, perched on a stool, was draping a muslin bodice straight onto Gill, our thirty-four hip model. A model's job is to stand still and be stabbed with pins.

"What are you wearing for Ascot? " Rachel asked me, head on one side admiring her gathers.

I thought she was making fun of me in front of Gill and didn't reply. When she repeated the question I felt hurt and in my head was mother's voice, "Our Mary, you let people walk all over you."

Holding the pin box steady I said timidly, "You know I'm not going."

She looked up, snatched a pin from between her teeth and snapped, "I should jolly well hope you are going to Ascot, Mr Cattell has ordered four tickets for us."

I was dumbstruck.

"Didn't you know?" she asked.

But I could not afford to go and would have to think of an excuse.

"Everything's paid for," said Rachel, mind reading and talking to the muslin, "entrance fees, dress allowance and out of pocket expenses."

How I loved Mr Cattell.

Then something terrible happened and all the excitement of the Ascot trip evaporated.

Jim, the caretaker, a big man with a broom, gave me six shillings and the names of three horses on a slip of paper. Betting was illegal at the time except on a racecourse and I agreed to put the money on the first name. If it won, the winnings were to go on the second horse and, if that won, I was to put every penny on the third and final horse. Rachel was furious when she heard about it, "We are not bookies' runners for caretakers." I felt dreadful as if I was being ungrateful and letting her down.

Mother	"You should have had more sense than to take his bet in the first place."
Dad	"Anyway, you're not old enough to bet on the tote, you have to be 21."
Mother	"There's your excuse. Give him the money back and say you're too young."
Me	"No."
Mother	"Why ever not?"

Me	"I promised, and the caretaker is nice to me, empties my basket first every morning."
Dad	"Well if that's how she feels Daisy, she'll have to do it. It's a free country."
Mother	"All right then but be discrete about it. When you get there make an excuse. Say you're going to find the Ladies then make your way to the Tote."
Me	"But I'll have to do that three times."
Dad	"No you won't. Just give the Tote the money and the horses' names, they'll see to it for you."
Mum	"Mind you keep the receipt."
Dad	"Well, that's all settled then."
Me	"What is the Tote?"

* * *

The parking field was the best bit. We'd set off early that fine morning in Rachel's car with our hats in Marshall and Snelgroves hatboxes and a packed lunch. Ascot race-goers traditionally picnic next to their cars on the grass before the first race at two o'clock. Everything was bright and colourful and the cut grass smelt wonderful.

Me	"Why is everybody looking at us?"
Rachel	"Not us. The car. They are looking at my car."

The red MG was open-topped with running boards and chrome bumpers and it was so old the key was lost and the ignition was turned with a nail file. Other cars were black and square and the one next to us had a chauffeur wearing leather gaiters. I could not stop myself from staring. From the boot, with help from another man, he unloaded a wicker hamper and opened it to reveal

Luxury goes with speed in the HUMBER Super Snipe

£985 plus p.t. £411.10.10
(Whitewall tyres extra).

Also
TOURING LIMOUSINE
(with sliding partition)
£1065 plus p.t. £444.17.6.

HILLMAN Estate Car

Farm Truck
or
Family Saloon

£540 plus p.t. £226.3.6.
(White-wall tyres, over-riders and chromium
windscreen available as extra).

THE Sunbeam
MK III SPORTS SALOON

£795 plus p.t. £331.7.6.
(Over-line white-wall tyres and over-riders
available as extra).

Sparkling performance—lower price

PRODUCTS OF THE ROOTES GROUP

Lansdowne Garage (Leicester) Ltd.
East Street, LEICESTER
TEL: GRANBY 966/7

The type of cars on Ascot car park. Advert from June 1955 Leicester Graphic.

knives and forks strapped in rows under the lid. Then they unloaded five wooden dining chairs and a table. I whispered to Rachel, "What sort of jobs would these people do?"

Rachel   "Jobs? These people don't work."

The men standing around the cars looked beautiful in their grey toppers and morning suits. They wore striped trousers and tailcoats with box pleats from the waist caught into grosgrain buttons. Tall men have a natural grace and they stood, holding white gloves behind their backs and balancing forward from the hips.

Using hatboxes as tables we ate our sandwiches pouring tea from flasks into china cups. Afterwards we took out the hats and spent ages putting them on. Rachel's was grey pleated silk to match her fitted coat and mine was a straw boater with daisies sewn round the crown to match the daisy in the lapel of my blue linen suit off the sample rail.

When we were ready to take photos somebody called, "This way please ladies," and a man from the group next to us stood up and raised his glass of champagne.

Some people came by the special train from London that terminated in the Ascot grounds and we watched them parading down the grass track to the grandstand. All the men were in grey and all the women were in a kind of uniform. This was either a dress and jacket or a suit of the colours found in Liquorice Allsorts, pinks, yellows, blues and greens. To complete the outfits their shoes, bags and wide-brimmed hats were of the same colour and must have been specially dyed to match. Skirts were either pencil slim or ballerina length and full. I did not know such people existed, they looked so happy and confident and unhurried.

As they neared the grandstand the crowd parted and women bent at the knee to curtsey as Princess Margaret passed through with her chums.

Me	"She's so petite and all that make-up."
Rachel	"That's for the newspaper photos."
Me	"She's the only one in a small hat."
Rachel	"That's because royalty has to be seen."

Rachel had placed a bet on a French horse called Belle de Jour and to shrieks of excitement it came in first. While she'd gone to collect her winnings I pushed through the crowd to see Belle de Jour come stamping and snorting into the winner's enclosure surrounded by men in trilbies clapping. It was strange to see all the lovely clothes next to the farmyard smell of steaming horse manure. Belle de Jour was a chestnut horse but every inch of her coat looked black and shiny with sweat. Her eyes were glaring and I spoke to a man in a trilby.

Me	"Is the horse ill?"
Man	"Good God I hope not!"
Me	"Why is she foaming at the mouth?"
Man	"She's excited because she's won."
Me	"Does she know she's won?"
Man	"They always know when they've won and they want to win again. If they lose a lot they get downhearted and have to be taken out for a few weeks."

* * *

By the time we were back in Leicester it was late and we called at my house for a cup of coffee because the tyres were flat and Rachel had to pump them up.

I ran in first to warn mother and to ask her to change her slippers and use the best cups.

Afterwards mother, speaking of Rachel, said, "I can't see anything in her, she's nothing special, she's just an ordinary girl." Mothers! What do they know?

Next morning I had to break the news to Big Jim that his first two horses won but it was all lost in the last race.

He carried on sweeping and didn't seem to mind at all. Dad said true gamblers expect to lose.

FITTING IN

Adapting speech to fit in with people in the design office was easy because for a long time I had been making seismic shifts in vowels every night in a drama group called the Moat Players.

The Moat Players in a scene from George Washington Slept Here.

As well as accents there were differences in vocabulary. Instead of 'mum and dad' art college people said 'my parents,' a phrase not used by factory girls who went home to 'get something to eat' rather than 'a meal.'

I learnt to buy birthday cards without glitter; they had to be plain and definitely no poems.

Another difference was in the matter of engagement rings. When girls in the factory became engaged their boyfriends saved up for months to buy the ring and everyone crowded round to admire it. The traditional ring at that time was gold with platinum shoulders and two or three diamonds so small they were barely visible. If the engagement was subsequently broken off the girl would return the ring but the jeweller would not take it back at any price and the boy would be lucky to be offered a fraction of its value from a dealer. Like dad said, 'workers are always robbed.'

But when Linda, a designer, and her architect boyfriend, became engaged, they chose a second-hand Victorian ring, with a garnet set in gold, paying far less than for a new ring and it would keep its value. The wedding was very different too.

Linda   "On the invitation my father is inviting the guests directly to the reception in a hotel. We will join them there after the registry office."

Me   "You're being married in a registry office?"

Linda   "Yes. Neither of us are churchgoers so it would be silly."

Me   "You know what the girls will think."

Linda   "They can think what they like."

This disregard for the opinion of others showed an enviable independence of mind. Girls in the factory cared what others thought of them and did not want to appear different. Anyone who was in the Girl Guides for instance or went to an evening class was considered rather odd.

Three friends, Thelma, Brenda and Sheila as models in a fashion show. I am on the right of the photograph and was the compere.

Linda invited me to her wedding reception and it was there I met Rachel's boyfriend, Martin. He was an artist, interested in stage design, and he wanted to know all about my drama group. Before long he joined and was building magnificent sets for us including one for *Brief Encounter* where the action took place in the buffet of a railway station.   .

In this way I was mixing with the art college crowd in the evenings as well as at work where we were making cotton dresses for summer.

One of my favourites was a royal blue linen with white spots as big as old pennies. I. and L. Stevens advertised this dress in *Vogue* magazine. It had cap sleeves, an open neck with high collar, fitted darts to the waist and a calf length skirt cut from a complete circle of material with a hole in the centre for the waist. Although it took an extravagant amount of cloth, and the hems were always tricky, the result was a wonderful flared movement over the stiff petticoat.

In the full-page black and white picture the model, Fiona Campbell-Waters, with her short, dark hair, was photographed in profile on a high stool. With the dress, she wore a small white hat, white high-heeled sandals and white cotton gloves. Nobody was dressed properly that year without little gloves. The whole picture spoke of summer elegance and, of course, it went on the design room wall along with all the other magazine pages.

A new word was entering the fashion lexicon – 'Casuals'. The style originated with American college girls and meant, not dresses, but separates, a skirt and matching unstructured top. In the factory they were called jumper suits. Two-piece suits in a tailored style had always been popular but these casuals were simple pull-on tops and skirts. They were easy to wear and easy to make, which, as it turned out, was not good, either for our firm or for the British fashion industry as a whole. I. and L. Stevens never made trousers, this fashion was to come – and stay, a few years later.

NEW YORK

Sylvia	"She's not coming, it's nearly ten."
Jane	"I've just seen her, she's here and she looks different."
Sylvia	"How d'ye mean?"
Jane	"Her skin. It's sort of glowing."
Mavis	"Where is she now?"
Jane	"Talking to Mr Cattell in his office, she'll be out soon."
Mavis	"Let's go and wait in the design office."
Jane	"I daren't do that."
Sylvia	"Yes we can, bring some work with you, think of something to ask her about it."
Jane	"It's all right for you, you're a sample hand – she'll tell us off."
Sylvia	"Come on, risk it."
Cath	"Can I come as well?"

Dress and Jacket **4½ gns.**

Wherever the warm
sun shines! Lovable
cottons by Horrockses.
On the left our two
in one. Button up for formal
occasions—catch the sun without
your jacket. On the right the
dress you'll wear with
happiness through Summer
days. **Both exclusive to
us in the Midlands.**
Sizes 34″– 40″
American sizes 10 -16.

Dress **79/6**

new
FOR YOU

Werff
BROTHERS LTD.

21 GALLOWTREE GATE, LEICESTER AND BRANCHES
Phone : Leicester 21176

*A fine example of 1950s style.
Advertisment from the
Leicester Graphic.*

The first day of January was a working day and the design office was crowded.

Rachel's parents were living in New York on business and they had sent for her to join them there for Christmas. On her return everybody wanted to know about New York

Rachel was not pleased to see so many people in her room but she looked too tired to do anything about it. Her skin looked lovely. She took off her coat and showed off her American dress with its black velvet bolero edged with dangling lace bobbles. The girls gathered round to feel the fabric and between sips of coffee Rachel said, "If you all knew what it was like none of you would stay here. Nobody sews and you can earn ten dollars just for turning a hem."

Sylvia, the sample machinist asked the question that none of us dare ask.

"Your complexion looks nice, what is it?"

"Moisturiser," said Rachel, "they don't use sticky creams in the States. Water is what the skin needs."

She told us about automat cafes where food was behind revolving glass and you put money in and took out any plate you fancied. She talked about something called 'pizza pie' and then she unwrapped a black beret with black sequins explaining that every major city has a rage and these berets were the rage of New York.

Me	"What's it made from?"
Rachel	"Angora."
Me	"Not the beret, this bag."
Rachel	"This is called polythene, everybody uses them, there are no paper bags there. See, it doesn't rip and it's waterproof."

We passed it round to feel its softness and strength. This beautiful polythene bag was possibly the first one seen in the city.

Rachel "Never mind the bag. Do you want to know about the clothes or not?"

Finding a stool or leaning against the tables we were ready. "Every dress in America is a step-in dress," she explained, "you can't sell a garment that has to be dragged over the head. In future we will do that here by using long back zips or front plackets."

Next she unwrapped something like a small box camera, "Press the button and look through," she said to Jane. "Now tell me what you can see." Jane could not speak. "Come along, pass it to Sylvia." Sylvia was also speechless. Then it was my turn. The box was a viewer for slides and it took my breath away. A 3D photo of a park, blue sky, deep snow, people skiing and it looked so real in the bright sunshine that you were there, right there in the middle of it. Rachel's mother, in the foreground, wearing a red coat that contrasted with the white, looked so close you could have lifted her up with one finger.

By now more workers were trying to manoeuvre themselves inside and taking turns at the viewer when Mr Cattell came in and announced:

"This is all very exciting but please go back to work ladies, Miss King is still recovering from her flight." As soon as they'd shuffled out he looked through the box and that night he took it home to show Mrs Cattell but not before it had been all round our factory and all round his brother-in-law's cigar factory upstairs.

TERESA

When Teresa told me she was not an assistant designer but a senior designer I did not believe her. Nobody believed Teresa. Her designs were not greatly original and her patterns were a joke. A piece that said, 'This side up' on the front also said "This side up' on the back, and ninety dresses had been cut wrongly. After that Rachel asked me to check all Teresa's patterns, which I was happy to do, even though it meant neglecting my own work. But when I discovered that she really was a senior designer and earning twice my salary all confidence in the value of my work evaporated.

When something niggles every day it eats away at the pleasure of a job.

Mother	"You should give your notice in and if they ask why you should tell them about Teresa."
Me	"I don't want to leave, I wouldn't be able to work anywhere else."
Dad	"Of course you can, you're as good as anybody."
Me	"I haven't got a diploma."
Mother	"Talent doesn't need a diploma, you'd soon get a better job. And nobody's appreciated in the place where they've learnt their trade."
Dad	"What does Teresa's father do?"

This was dad's standard question for all my acquaintances and the one he judged people by.

Me	"He owns a big firm, he makes fabrics."

Photograph taken at Jerome's Studio Granby Street, Leicester, aged 20.

Dad   "Oh, one of Mr Cattell's pals is he? That's how she got the job. They wouldn't allow that in Russia."

In the end Mum said I should ask Mr Cattell for a rise.

It was all very worrying but after two weeks I made an appointment with him and stood waiting at his door rehearsing my speech.

"Do sit down Mary," he said, "I think I know why you are here."

I'd mentioned the appointment to Rachel because Dad told me it was wrong to go over anybody's head. She said, "You must do what you want to do."

Waiting till he'd shaken his Swan Vestas box to see if there were any matches left and then waiting till he'd filled his pipe from a tin of Three Nuns tobacco and set it alight, I began by saying how much I enjoyed the work and asking why my pay was a lot less than Teresa's. The room was soon full of the woody smoke that I liked.

After a few thoughtful puffs Mr Cattell said it would be improper to discuss the salary of anyone else and there were always anomalies in wages. Then the pipe went out and he lit it again and tidied his desk while I waited. He said he would change my title from assistant designer to designer and he would be pleased to give me a rise but it would not correspond to the wages of a college-trained person because there was always an extra emolument for a diploma.

 As I was leaving he said, "We wouldn't like to lose you, you know," and I replied, "Of course not Sir."

I'm not sure what I expected from that interview but I came away feeling more miserable than when I went in.

NEW BOYFRIEND

Not long after this, and overnight, the world became another place because I had a new boyfriend who knew about opera and wine. He was better looking than the art college boys and older, with a car, even if the roof leaked. Foreign, and therefore classless, Jewish, and therefore a citizen of the world.

We met at the Palais de Danse, where, on Thursdays, there were evening dress dances sponsored by local manufacturers but open to the public. That night it was the annual Candy Ball for the confectionery industry and, wearing a black georgette three-quarter length dress, I went with my parents and brother. A man asked me to dance, which was surprising, because I was talking to my brother at the time, but he looked nice, with dark hair, dark eyes and a friendly expression so I agreed. He said he was twenty-nine and from Czechoslovakia.

Everybody attending the ball had been given a box of confectionery. He wanted to know what was in my box and when I said "Black Magic" he asked if I'd swap them for his Liquorice Allsorts. When I said they were hidden behind a curtain he said he'd done the same and could we make the change over after the dance. We danced again and then I took him to the balcony to meet my family.

When I introduced him to Mum and Dad he clicked his heels and made a little bow. I could tell by the way they glanced at each other that they were impressed.

Later, when mother stood up to look over the balcony he leapt to his feet.

"Oh," said mother, "are you leaving us?"

"Don't be silly Daisy," said Dad, "he's not going anywhere. He's standing up because you are."

In his car on the way home he made a confession,

Aged 21 with borrowed kitten.

"I'm not twenty-nine, I'm thirty and I'm not from Czechoslovakia, I'm from Germany."

Next day my new dance partner called at the factory and I introduced him to Rachel. When he'd gone, I waited for the usual cynical comments she created for my boyfriends, creepy caterpillars and so forth. Instead she made an announcement to the design office, "Did you notice how he put his jacket on, over the shoulders first, like a cape, that's the continental way. And did you see him click his heels?"

One night, mother, who'd been waiting up for me watching the television, newly rented for the forthcoming coronation, was making me a cup of tea in the kitchen. I took my coat off slowly, hung it over the newel post at the bottom of the stairs and settled myself at the breakfast table before calling to her.

Me   "I might marry this man."

Mother (calling back) "You are a funny thing. You've only known him three weeks."

Me   "Two."

Mother (calling) "D'ye want a biscuit?"

Me   "He's coming tomorrow to ask you for my hand."

Mother   "Oh."

Me   "I mean it."

Mother (dashing in from the kitchen with the tray) "Oh, dear I'd better wake your dad up."

Me   "And he's Jewish."

Mother (putting the tray down)   "Oh! You can forget all about that you silly girl. He won't marry you. They never marry out of their religion. And did you tell him we have no money?"

* * *

Now it was my turn to be engaged, and the girls crowded round to admire the Victorian ring with five amethysts from an antique shop in Stamford. When I told Rachel I was engaged she said, "Well, as long as he's kind to you, that's what matters." I thought this was a strange remark and still do. It was so unromantic.

Rachel was now renting an Elizabethan vicarage and she seemed quite taken with my fiancé.

Rachel   "Will you bring him if I invite you to a picnic in the grounds and does he eat Walkers pork sausages?"

Me   "He *only* eats Walker's pork sausages."

That summer the two of us were often invited out with Rachel's friends, usually to the stately homes that were newly open to the public. Everywhere else was closed on Sundays and trips to these country mansions with their architecture and paintings were extremely popular. Rachel laughed a lot with my fiancé and they made up silly jokes together in French.

Although we were meeting socially I was still in awe of Rachel and conscious of the teacher and pupil basis of the friendship. After a lot of thought I decided to broach the subject of my wedding dress. What I really wanted was for her to design it and I chose an afternoon when Rachel was sitting with French Vogue and I was unpicking some pleats.

Me   "What kind of wedding dress shall I choose?"

Rachel   "What do you want?"

The Wedding Dress.

Me   "Something that doesn't date."

Rachel   "All fashion will date."

I said no more thinking the conversation was at an end but after a while she said, "Follow the line of the body, that never changes."

Me   "What about material?"

Rachel   "Which month?"

Me   "July."

Rachel   "Cotton lace over cambric, three-quarter length skirt."

Me (trying to sound casual)   "Is a high neck right for summer?"

Rachel   "No, a round neck cut low with narrow shoulders and a high necked bolero of the same material. At least ten front buttons with shanks. And loop buttonholes. Pass me that pencil."

The cotton lace dress was made in the factory two days later from material on Leicester market. The veil cut from a yard of tulle, was embroidered on the Cornelli machine. I think the whole lot cost two pounds ten shillings.

I thought Rachel was joking when she said her crowd had booked themselves into our honeymoon guesthouse in Cornwall, but it was true. Eight of us for breakfast every morning.

* * *

Back in Leicester, my new husband, calling in the factory one day, was surprised to be told I was out shopping for Rachel. That evening he said, "My wife doesn't shop for anybody, ask Mr Cattell for a reference and get yourself a proper designer's job."

So I did.

END PIECE

Modelling a Marks and Spencer dress made by S.M. Hurst at Wigston. 1955.

S.M. Hurst at Wigston doubled my salary when I went there to design mass-produced dresses for Marks and Spencers to the most exacting standards.

Regular inspections by an M & S team, who rolled down West Avenue in a chauffeured Daimler, checked there were no fewer than ten stitches to the inch and no deviation from the sample.

The designs were not greatly exciting because they had to look good on a hanger and have general appeal, but this level of factory control resulted in high quality affordable fashion unrivalled anywhere.

A few years later I gave up designing to be at home with my children and to spend more time with a drama group.

Most things in life happen by chance, and in 1964 I switched off the iron one afternoon to make a phone call.

I rang Marie Villiers, a Little Theatre friend, to ask if I could watch her give a drama lesson. Marie was teaching drama two hours a week at South Fields College, now Leicester College.

"Oh, no dear," she said, "that's not possible, no teacher wants anyone watching."

Me	"Sorry. I wish I hadn't asked you."
Marie	"No need to apologize dear. It's funny you should ring because I'm thinking of giving it up. You would be just the person to take over."

Me   "I couldn't do that, I'm not qualified."

Marie   "That doesn't matter dear, you've had lots of drama experience and they'd be interested in costume making as well."

Me   "The thought of teaching terrifies me."

Marie   "There's a teacher shortage, you could do it."

So began twenty-five wonderful years as a full time English and Drama lecturer in Further Education, among the exciting company of young people.

During that time, Harold Wilson, of blessed memory, created the Open University where people like me who had missed out could take a degree in such life-enhancing subjects as literature, music and philosophy.

One afternoon during a break in a garden bridge game, I was talking with three women friends, who were also retired, about our first jobs when one of them said, "I never speak about my first job."

Me   "Why not?"

Anne (with a shudder) "Oh. No, that's a part of my life that's long gone."

Me   "What did you do?"

Anne   "If you must know I worked in a factory making socks. There, I've said it!"

Me   "What's wrong with that?"

Anne   "Oh, you don't tell anybody you worked in a factory, it was a low job. My life's different now."

The Leicester knitwear industry has all but vanished and I thought of the generations of skilled workers making dresses, jumpers, underwear and socks.

How many like Anne, I wondered, were now ashamed of what they perceived as lowly work.

She was right of course, factory work was for the poor and uneducated. Factory workers were considered 'common'. It made me think of all the beautiful girls who worked alongside me in a factory and the fun we had. And none of them were common.

That night I started to write a few pages about my work.... and that's how this book came about.

Leicestershire Legends

retold by Black Annis

'Let's you and I get a thing or two straight. The name's Black Annis, but you may call me 'Cat Anna' between yourselves – but not to my face, if you value the appearance of yours. There've been days when the aches and pains make me a bit awkward at times, I'll admit as much myself. I've been known to get a bit upset when silly little kids used to play around outside my cave and shout rude remarks like me being an old witch.'

But is she or isn't she? Just an old woman with an attitude problem or actually more of a witch? Herself one of Leicester's best-known legends, Black Annis never quite lets on if she really knows more than she is prepared to say about the Old Ways. But in her direct manner, and with a bit of help from some of her friends, she retells some of the tales of Leicestershire in a way they've never been heard before, with local phrases and dialect rather than written out all posh.

Phantom black hounds, weird goings on where saints were murdered, very odd ways of finding water, pipers who enter underground tunnels and are never seen again, stories about stones, strange lights in the sky, and any number of ghosts – it's all happened in Leicestershire and much more besides, at least if these legends are to be believed.

Specially illustrated by Jenny Clarke, one of Britain's leading tattoo designers.

ISBN 1872883 77 X. 2004. Demi 8vo (215 x 138 mm), 99 + xiv pages, 10 line drawings, perfect bound. **£6.95**

Also published by Heart of Albion Press

Rutland Village by Village

Bob Trubshaw

A guide to the history of all the villages in Rutland, with the emphasis on places that can be seen or visited. Based on the author's sixteen years of research into the little-known aspects of the county.

ISBN 1 872883 69 9. 2003, demi 8vo (215 x 138 mm), 73 + x pages, 53 b&w photos, perfect bound. **£6.95**

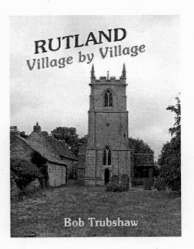

Little-Known Leicestershire and Rutland

Bob Trubshaw

Drawing upon nearly ten years of research into the holy wells, standing stones, medieval carvings and crosses of the county, this book gives 12 circular bicycle or car routes around unspoiled countryside. Introductory chapters are provided for those less familiar with these topics.

ISBN 1 872 883 40 0. 1995, A5, perfect bound, 128 pages, 9 photos, 14 maps, 49 drawings. **£6.95**

Also published by Heart of Albion Press

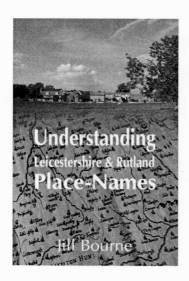

Understanding Leicestershire and Rutland Place-Names

Jill Bourne

We take for granted the names we use for places. Yet these names are a valuable part of our cultural heritage, providing a detailed insight into the early history of the region. Place-names reveal the otherwise lost voices of our forebears who settled here.

Understanding Leicestershire and Rutland Place-Names analyses the whole range of place-names which occur in Leicestershire and Rutland, most of which were coined between 1,000 and 1,500 years ago. These place-names describe, often in fine detail, the landscape, geology, rivers, buildings, flora, fauna, boundaries, meeting places, roads and track-ways. This book also looks at the distribution of the names, the languages from which they are derived, the successive waves of conquerors and migrants who fought and settled here, and the society they created.

Jill Bourne is an historian, archaeologist and museum professional who has specialised in the area of place-name studies and landscape history for over 20 years.

ISBN 1872883 71 0. 2003, perfect bound. Demi 8vo (215 x 138 mm), 145 + viii pages, 5 maps. **£6.95**

Also published by Heart of Albion Press

Sepulchral Effigies of Leicestershire and Rutland

Text by Max Wade Matthews

Photographs by Bob Trubshaw

This CD-ROM makes available for the first time details of the wealth of sepulchral effigies in Leicestershire and Rutland - from thirteenth century priests, thorough alabaster knights in armour and their ladies, to the splendours of seventeenth century Classical aggrandisement. There are even a number of twentieth century effigies too.

350 photos depict 141 effigies in 72 churches, all with detailed descriptions and useful hypertext indexes. Runs on PCs and Macs.

ISBN 1 872883 54 0 **£14.95** incl. VAT.

Special offer!

Mail order customers save 17.5% (because Heart of Albion is not VAT registered) = **£12.70**

Also published by Heart of Albion Press

Interactive Little-known Leicestershire and Rutland

Text and photographs by Bob Trubshaw

For seventeen years the author has been researching the 'little-known' aspects of Leicestershire and Rutland. Topics include holy wells, standing stones and mark stones, medieval crosses, and a wide variety of Romanesque and medieval figurative carvings - and a healthy quota of 'miscellaneous' sites.

Some of this information appeared in early Heart of Albion publications (mostly long out of print), but this CD-ROM contains extensive further research. The information covers 241 parishes and includes no less than 550 'large format' colour photographs (all previously unpublished).

There are introductory essays, a glossary and plenty of hypertext indexes.

Runs on PCs and Macs.
ISBN 1 872883 53 2. **£14.95** incl. VAT.

Special offer!

Mail order customers save 17.5% (because Heart of Albion is not VAT registered) = **£12.70**

Interactive Gargoyles and Grotesque Carvings of Leicestershire and Rutland

Text and photographs
by Bob Trubshaw

A selection of images from *Interactive Little-known Leicestershire and Rutland* for those particularly interested in Romanesque and medieval figurative carvings. No less than 240 photos – including plenty of Green Men, tongue-pokers and a wide variety of other grotesques. Introductory text, glossary and plenty of hypertext indexes.

Runs on PCs and Macs.

ISBN 1 872883 57 5 **£11.75** incl. VAT.

Special offer! Because Heart of Albion is not VAT registered mail order customers save 17.5 percent = **£10.00**

Musical Leicester

Max Wade Matthews

There was an amazing diversity of music-making in Leicester during the eighteenth and nineteenth centuries, involving many nationally and internationally renowned performers. *Musical Leicester* describes the evolution of such diverse forms of music-making as 'classical' music concerts, minstrel troupes, oratorios, local orchestras, brass bands, bell ringing, organists and church choirs.

Many notable citizens contributed their energy and enthusiasm to the growth and success of music-making in Leicester, although almost all of them are now unjustly forgotten.

Max Wade-Matthews' research reveals many aspects of Leicester's history that would otherwise have remained overlooked. The detailed information on the concerts, musicians, promoters and venues, combined with a lively style of writing, ensures that *Musical Leicester* will inform and entertain all those interested in music making, social history and local history.

Undoubtedly this will be of immense value to anyone interested in the cultural development of the modern city as it is a mine of information about all sorts of musical activities that have long been forgotten and of some that are still going strong today... Altogether this book is a treasure house of musical history – highly recommended.
Leicester Mercury

ISBN 1 872883 51 6. 1998. A5, 253 pages, 43 b&w photos, 58 line drawings, full colour laminated cover, perfect bound. **£14.95**

Cinema in Leicester 1896–1931

David Williams

Thorough research into the early cinemas of the city; fully illustrated.

An enormously detailed and extensively illustrated survey of cinema in Leicester from the earliest times... Meticulously researched... destined to become the definitive work on the subject. It is also an enjoyable and entertaining read...
Leicestershire Historian

ISBN 1 872883 20 6. 1993, A5, 260 pages, 233 illustrations, perfect bound. **£12.95**

Further details of all Heart of Albion titles online at
www.hoap.co.uk

All titles available direct from Heart of Albion Press.
Please add £1.30 p&p (UK only; email
albion@indigogroup.co.uk for overseas postage).

To order books or request our current catalogue please
contact

Heart of Albion Press

2 Cross Hill Close, Wymeswold
Loughborough, LE12 6UJ

Phone: 01509 880725
Fax: 01509 881715
email: albion@indigogroup.co.uk
Web site: www.hoap.co.uk

Edición original de Mango Jeunesse
Título original: *Le petit manchot*
© 2005, Mango Jeunesse
© 2006, de esta edición, Combel Editorial, S.A.
Casp, 79 – 08013 Barcelona
Tel.: 902 107 007
Adaptación: Fina Palomares
Segunda edición: abril 2009
ISBN: 978-84-9825-131-9

Printed in France by Pollina - L50085B

¿Quién eres?

El pingüino

Textos de Anne Jonas

Combel
EDITORIAL

Al calor de papá

¡Crac, crac! Al igual que otros polluelos sobre el hielo, el pequeño pingüino ha roto la cáscara bajo la atenta mirada de su padre. Y es que éste ya lleva casi dos meses incubando el huevo sin perderlo de vista ni un solo instante. Y la madre, ¿dónde está? Una vez pone el huevo, va al mar en busca de comida para su cría. Y volverá, claro que volverá. En pocos días ya estará de vuelta.

Aunque el pequeño pingüino sea un ave marina, nace lejos del mar, pues los pingüinos forman colonias en tierra firme. Todavía tienen que pasar muchos meses antes de que se sumerja en el agua.

TÚ, ¿QUÉ OPINAS?

¿Por qué el pequeño pingüino se queda entre las patas de su padre tras nacer?

→ Respuesta 1: Porque es muy perezoso.

→ Respuesta 2: Porque no sabe caminar.

→ Respuesta 3: Porque tiene frío.

3

Los polluelos nacen en la parte más fría de la Tierra: en los témpanos de los glaciares. Allí la temperatura es de –50 °C, es decir, hace más frío que en el congelador de casa. Por eso, se quedan bien cobijados entre las patas de papá hasta que reúnen fuerzas suficientes y... ¡les salen plumas! Eso sí, de vez en cuando, sacan la cabeza de su refugio para observar el gran desierto blanco que los rodea.

Al principio, sólo los protege un plumón gris, lanoso y opaco, que poco a poco van perdiendo porque en su lugar salen plumas.

las patas de su padre porque tiene frío.

En cambio, cuando es adulto, una gruesa capa de grasa y un plumaje denso e impermeable lo protegen del frío.

Para que no se les congele la punta de las patas, los pingüinos descansan sobre su pequeña cola y sobre los talones.

Si sale el sol, los pingüinos exponen a él su dorso de color negro. Así logran almacenar algo de calor, sobre todo cuando incuban.

Ya viene mamá

¡Por fin ha llegado el gran día! Mamá ya está aquí. Es el momento de reencontrarse con papá y de conocer al pequeño. El camino es larguísimo porque los pingüinos ponen el huevo a unos cien kilómetros del mar. En coche, tardaríamos una hora en recorrer el trayecto. En cambio, los pingüinos tardan un mes aproximadamente porque sus patas son muy cortas y porque, a pesar de ser aves, no vuelan.

Cuando nacen los pequeños, los pingüinos se arremolinan entre ellos formando un círculo para guardar el calor.

TÚ, ¿QUÉ OPINAS?

Mamá pingüino, ¿cómo reconoce a papá pingüino?

→ Respuesta 1: Por su llamada.

→ Respuesta 2: Por las plumas.

→ Respuesta 3: Por su manera de balancearse.

6

Es difícil reconocer a un macho entre miles de pingüinos vestidos con el mismo traje negro y blanco. Por eso, la única solución es que la hembra rodee al grupo y emita un sonido particular que él reconocerá y responderá. Y es que no hay dos pingüinos que realicen la misma llamada.

Cuando vuelve del mar, la hembra lleva consigo hasta tres kilos de pescado y de langostinos en una especie de bolsa que tiene entre la boca y el estómago.

Mientras, papá pingüino calma el hambre de su pequeño con una sustancia lechosa que regurgita y le pone dentro del pico.

8

papá pingüino por su llamada.

¡Qué poco dura el feliz encuentro! Una vez que la hembra vuelve, el macho se va al mar.
¡Ya lleva cuatro meses ingiriendo sólo nieve!

¡A la guardería todos!

El pequeño pingüino tiene ahora seis semanas. Ha crecido y su cuerpo se ha cubierto de un plumón espeso. Ya puede salir del cobijo de la madre y aventurarse por el hielo. Pasados unos cuantos días más, sus padres se irán juntos hacia el mar. Mientras, los pequeños pingüinos se agrupan entre sí en una especie de guardería, vigilada por algunos adultos.

Los pequeños esperan la llegada de los padres y, cuando lo hacen, los reconocen por su llamada. Ellos les contestan de igual forma.

TÚ, ¿QUÉ OPINAS?

¿Por qué los pingüinos ponen el huevo lejos del mar?

→ Respuesta 1: Para protegerse del viento.

→ Respuesta 2: Porque tienen miedo de que los polluelos caigan al agua.

→ Respuesta 3: Porque les gusta viajar lejos.

Aunque no sople tan fuerte como cerca del mar, el viento puede alcanzar una velocidad de doscientos kilómetros por hora. Durante las ventiscas, las ráfagas de viento arremolinan cristales de hielo que se clavan como millones de pequeñas agujas. Para protegerse de ellas, los pingüinos se acurrucan entre sí.

12

El camino hacia el mar es largo para estas aves que caminan con dificultad sobre sus cortas patas.

lejos del mar para protegerse del viento.

El pingüino camina balanceándose sobre sus patas palmípedas.
Su andar se parece al del payaso que lleva los pantalones caídos hasta el tobillo.

¡Cuidado porque el hielo resbala! Afortunadamente, las garras fuertes de sus patas impiden que puedan caerse.

¡Anda, una pendiente! Los pingüinos la aprovechan y bajan por ella en luge: se desplazan sobre el abdomen, empujando con las alas y las patas. ¡Es menos cansado que caminar, claro!

13

Y muy pronto... ¡a sumergirse!

Los pequeños pingüinos están preparados para sumergirse. Recorren el camino que lleva al mar junto con sus padres. Allí podrán jugar con las olas y comer todo el pescado, gambas y langostinos que quieran. En cuanto entren en el agua, sabrán nadar y alimentarse como si fueran adultos.

Los polluelos tienen ahora cinco meses. Es el momento de cambiar el plumón lanoso por plumas.

TÚ, ¿QUÉ OPINAS?

¿Qué hace un pingüino antes de sumergirse?

→ Respuesta 1: Ahueca las plumas.

→ Respuesta 2: Comprueba que no haya ningún animal peligroso en el agua.

→ Respuesta 3: Comprueba la temperatura del agua con la punta de la pata.

15

Poca maña en tierra firme pero en el agua... todo cambia: el pingüino es el ave marina más rápida. A pesar de sus excelentes facultades como nadador, debe tener mucho cuidado con el leopardo marino, pariente de la foca, y con la orca, familia del delfín. Cuando atacan al pingüino, éste nada cambiando constantemente de dirección para desorientar a su rival e intenta salir del agua lo más rápido posible.

Para sumergirse, los pingüinos se deslizan sobre el abdomen y se tiran en plancha al agua.

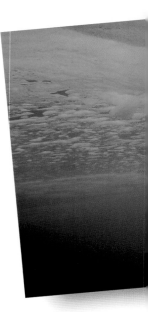

ningún animal peligroso en el agua.

Al igual que los delfines, los pingüinos nadan saltando sobre las olas para cansarse menos. Tras salir del agua, se propulsan sobre el hielo.

Cuando pesca, el pingüino selecciona a su presa: langostinos, gambas, pescado, calamares... Después, la persigue y la coge con el pico.

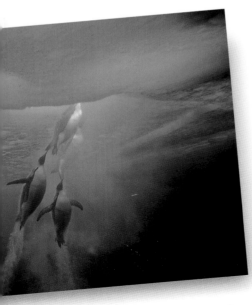

Como un buceador de primera, el pingüino persigue a su presa hasta 250 metros de profundidad. Puede estar veinte minutos en el agua sin respirar.

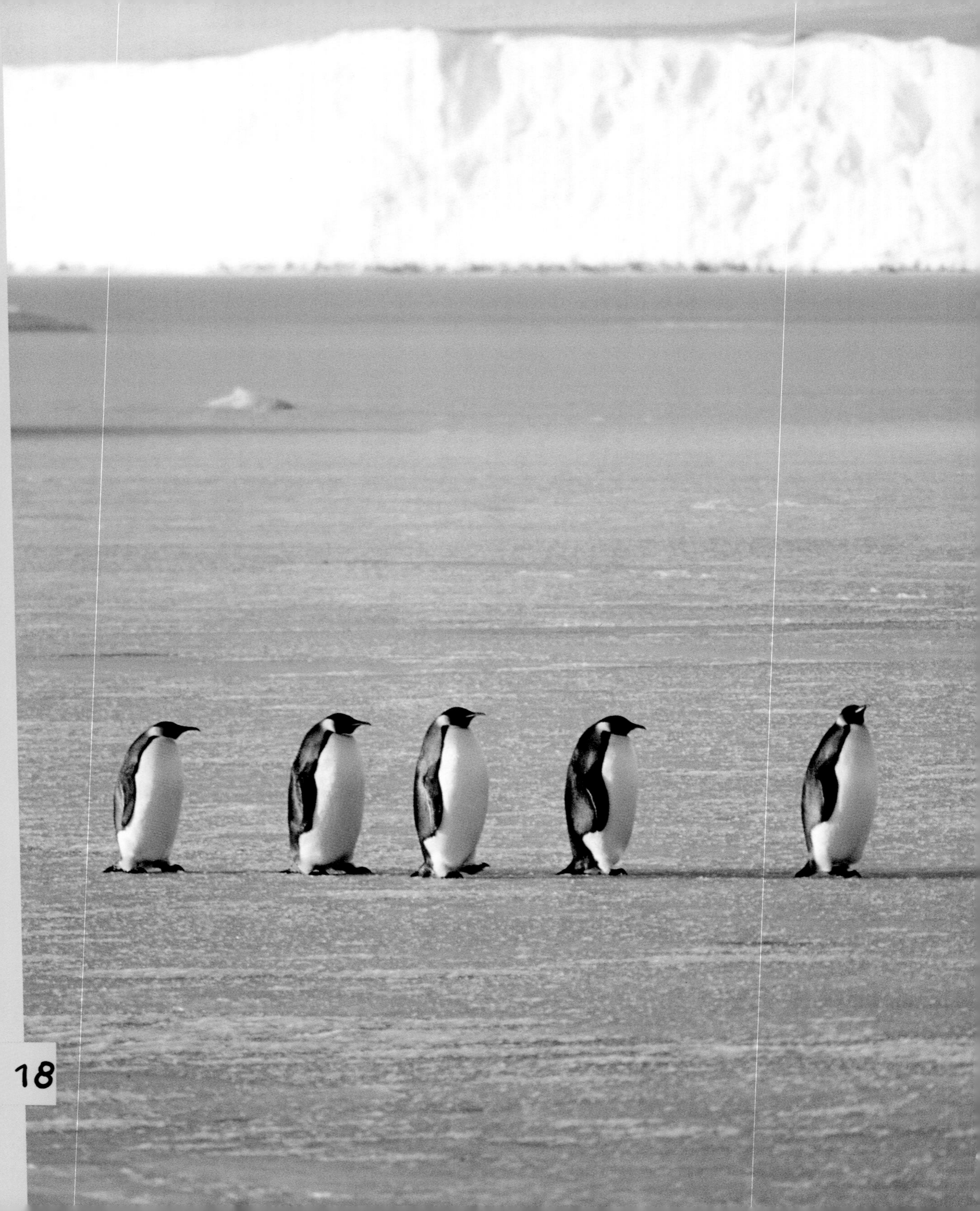

¡De nuevo en tierra!

Tras dos meses nadando y comiendo pescado, es el momento de volver a tierra firme. El pequeño pingüino es ahora adulto. Vuelve al lugar donde nació para formar una nueva familia. ¡Ya han llegado todos! Las hembras rodean la colonia para elegir a un macho. Para seducir a una hembra, los machos realizan exhibiciones, levantando las alas, inclinándose y emitiendo una llamada. La pareja sólo tendrá un huevo, que será incubado por el macho.

Los pingüinos emprenden un largo viaje por el glaciar sin perderse... ¡y por el camino más corto!

TÚ, ¿QUÉ OPINAS?

¿Qué hacen los pingüinos para calentarse mientras incuban?

→ Respuesta 1: Corren alrededor del huevo.

→ Respuesta 2: Aletean.

→ Respuesta 3: Se acurrucan entre sí.

¡Es imposible hacer un nido en el hielo del glaciar! No hay nada para ello. Los machos que incuban el huevo, pues, no pueden dejarlo ni un instante porque se helaría. Para entrar en calor, se agrupan entre sí y establecen turnos en los que los pingüinos del interior pasan al exterior de la formación y viceversa.

Durante los dos meses de incubación, los pingüinos pueden llegar a perder la mitad de su peso.

20

El macho tiene un pliegue abdominal entre sus cortas patas que le sirve de bolsa para incubar el huevo y cuidar la cría. En ella la temperatura es superior a los 30 °C.

entre sí para calentarse.

Una vez que la hembra ha puesto el huevo, se lo pasa cuidadosamente con las patas al macho sin que toque el hielo ni un solo instante, pues sería mortal para el pequeño.

El pingüino emperador es un ave: su cuerpo está cubierto de plumas y se reproduce mediante huevos. Pertenece al orden de los esfenisciformes: no vuela pero nada. La familia de los pingüinos está formada por diecisiete especies, entre ellos el pingüino real, algo más pequeño que el pingüino emperador, y el pingüino de penacho anaranjado. Su nombre científico es *Aptenodytes forsteri:* todos los animales poseen un nombre en latín, conocido por todos los científicos. El pingüino emperador adulto pesa entre 23 y 38 kilos. Vive en las barreras del hielo y en los icebergs del continente antártico, un territorio deshabitado de 14 millones de km², cubierto de nieve todo el año.

Hay muchos animales y todos ellos bien diferentes. Por eso, los científicos los han clasificado en función de sus diferencias y semejanzas.

Desde la cabeza hasta las patas, el pingüino emperador mide 1,10 m aproximadamente. ¡Lo mismo que un niño de siete años!

El pingüino no puede volar. Sus alas se han transformado en aletas nadadoras, rígidas y planas.

Utiliza a menudo las plumas rígidas de su cola a modo de tercera pata.

Su pico es largo, puntiagudo y ligeramente curvo en su extremo; presenta una franja de color al lado. La lengua es espinosa y sus mandíbulas muy fuertes, lo que les permite atrapar fácilmente a sus presas.

Presenta tonos de color naranja a ambos lados del cuello.

Su dorso está cubierto de plumas negras impermeables; el abdomen es blanco.

En sus patas hay unas fuertes garras, que le permiten aferrarse al hielo.

23

Créditos de fotografía

Títulos de la colección